NEW DIRECTIONS

A Competitive Intelligence Tale

NEW DIRECTIONS

A Competitive Intelligence Tale

Gary D. Maag and David J. Kalinowski

ISBN 978-1-257-99582-0

Contents

INTRODUCTION

According to some recent business publications, *The World Is Flat* (and becoming hot and crowded), there are *Barbarians at the Gate*, and fundamental missteps prevent most companies from making the leap from *Good* to *Great*. But you already knew all that, didn't you?

What you probably don't know is something the most influential business books of the past decade haven't told you: competitive intelligence will be essential to the future success of any business.

Ask yourself, how well does your company gather, analyze, and take action based on what it knows about the competition? Sure, your market research department has a decent budget and a capable team, but the intelligence generated through traditional market research is firmly rooted in the past and present. It can tell you what your competitors have done and what they're currently doing, but it will leave you in the dark when it comes to the future. And when your company is making multimillion-dollar investments in new products and services, being in the dark about the competition is the last place you want to be. Having even the briefest of glimpses of the future can be a godsend in the planning and decision-making processes, and only one tool can offer such a glimpse: competitive intelligence.

"Hold on a second," you say, "my company doesn't engage in the cloak-and-dagger stuff." Good, because if cloak-and-dagger business tactics aren't illegal, they're almost certainly unethical. And competitive intelligence is neither of those two things.

Competitive intelligence, by definition, is the use of legal and ethical means to gather, analyze, and act upon relevant business information about the competition. It is not the clandestine, midnight-rendezvous, secret-handshake activity some believe it to be. It's not about breaking into Coca-Cola's vault to find the secret formula; it's about conducting hard-core primary research to find the trails of bread crumbs all companies leave throughout the supply chain when they conduct business in the global economy. Think investigative journalist versus CIA agent, or a sports team scouting the opposition versus breaking into the locker room to swipe the playbook.

So, why now? Why, at this point in time, is something that's been around formally for nearly thirty years (informally since the dawn of capitalism) so important to the future success of your business? Because competitive intelligence is at a critical juncture. The practice has matured to the point where, like any established profession, guidelines and best practices have been developed and tested to produce the best results—not to mention the best return on investment (ROI). Much like the early days of the public relations and advertising industries, competitive intelligence is gradually proving its value, and businesses from all industries are beginning to take notice. The competitive intelligence seed has been planted and nourished, and it's now beginning to grow.

Two other factors are making competitive intelligence an absolutely essential discipline: information technology (IT) and the contemporary business environment. Competitive intelligence as a field is taking full advantage of IT advances to gather intel, create analytical models, and engage in business wargaming. And changing business dynamics—from mergers and acquisitions to globalization to changes in the regulatory environment—have intensified the need for intelligence that effectively impacts business decisions.

The business stars are aligned. Now is the time to embrace competitive intelligence, because before long, you'll be reading influential business books all about the successful, forward-thinking companies that did.

To further explore the concept and benefits of competitive intelligence, we invite you to join us as we follow the experiences of "Jack Turner," a fictional market research executive who learns how to master the power of CI to help his industry-leading company beat back a challenge for number-one status from an aggressive, nimble competitor. Business readers in all industries can follow the lessons Jack Turner learns as he demonstrates how to use and apply CI to advance a firm's strategic priorities.

PART 1

WHEN IT RAINS:
AN ONSLAUGHT OF EVENTS

CHAPTER 1

JACK

Jack Turner got the call during his morning commute. Howard Hewitt, the founder and patriarch of Hewitt Games, was dead.

After the initial shock and disbelief of the news faded, Jack's first thought—like every other employee at the video game console developer's Chicago headquarters that Tuesday morning—was, *What now?*

Hewitt was an iconic figure in the industry, among the very first to bring video games into the home in the early 1980s. And while consoles from various competitors had come and gone over the years, Hewitt's Primo remained. In its nearly thirty-year history, the numerous incarnations of the popular device had never fallen below second place in the market.

It was an astounding run, and if you asked any one of Hewitt's 6,212 employees to pinpoint exactly how the company was able to achieve such a feat, the response would come without hesitation: Howard Hewitt.

"The man was a machine," Jack said, sitting in front of the cluttered desk of his friend and colleague Andy Barrows.

"A liquid metal terminator is more like it," Barrows replied. "It's not tough to understand why his heart gave out. The man just never stopped. And if you ever got in his way, watch out."

The two men grinned, remembering personal experiences with the brilliant but often maniacal Howard Hewitt, the man *Fortune* once profiled with the accurate headline "The Bobby Knight of Business."

"You want to know how to stay on top in this game?" Barrows said, perfectly imitating Hewitt's booming voice. "Don't sleep. I gave it up years ago, and it's worked wonders for me."

"You joke, but it's true," Jack said with a smile. "My team got back from a two-week China trip a few years back, and the time difference just killed me. After the second night of tossing and turning in bed, driving Sofia nuts, I finally decided to just come into the office. I pull into the garage—got in just before 4:00 AM—and whose Mercedes did I see parked next to the elevator?"

"Hewitt's," Barrows said.

Jack nodded. "I figured he must have left it overnight for some reason. Out of curiosity, I felt the hood. The engine was still warm."

"I told you," Barrows said, picking up the impersonation, "I gave up sleep years ago—had 'em install a hyperbaric chamber in my office."

Jack laughed, thankful for his friend's trademark wit on this dark day. The two had met as undergrads at Northwestern University and had become fast friends. It was Barrows who worked his way into Hewitt Games first, parlaying a dream summer internship into a full-time position and paving the way for Jack to follow. Nearly twelve years later, both men had climbed the corporate ladder, with Barrows as Hewitt's director of human resources and Jack the company's director of market research.

"He was a one of a kind," Jack said.

"Broke the mold." Barrows added. Both men sat in silence for a moment.

"What now?" Jack finally asked.

"That's what I've been asking myself all morning. I just can't imagine Hewitt Games without Howard Hewitt."

Jack expelled a deep breath. "Neither can I, my friend. Neither can I."

CHAPTER 2

THE MYSTERY MAN

It was a surreal day at Hewitt Games. Jack Turner, Andy Barrows, and the rest of the company's employees went about their jobs in a daze. Gazing out the window appeared to have become a key function of every position.

As each hour passed, it became increasingly obvious that Hewitt's energetic, hands-on approach to management, and his near omnipresence within the company he'd built, was the spark that kept the entire organization running at peak performance.

And the question remained, hanging over every employee's head: *What now?* There was no Number Two at Hewitt Games; there was Howard Hewitt, founder, president, and CEO, and then there was everyone else. Strangely, though, one name continually popped up among the speculation: Bob Laurence.

Laurence was a close confidant of Hewitt's with a sizable office on the top floor and the nondescript title of "vice president." Vice president of exactly what, no one could say. Bob Laurence was a mystery, and that only fueled the scuttlebutt.

Some claimed that the two men had served together in Vietnam. Laurence had saved Hewitt's life during the Tet Offensive, the story went, and Hewitt had repaid Laurence with a cushy job with no real responsibility. Others claimed Laurence was Hewitt's personal biographer, chronicling the great man's life for a future best seller. The most outlandish claim pegged Laurence as a Svengali of sorts, using secret knowledge to exercise control over Hewitt for an ultimately sinister purpose.

Jack was among the few employees at the company who had actually spoken with Laurence. The conversations were always brief, over the phone, and they were always in regard to Jack's latest market research and analytical work. Exactly what

Laurence did with the reports, Jack couldn't say. And other than that, Jack was in the dark. On a whim, he decided to look up Laurence in the company's internal directory, and he was surprised to see that Laurence's name wasn't listed.

He called the front desk to see if they could connect him. After a moment on hold, the receptionist came back on the line and said Laurence was no longer with the company.

"Do you know when he left?" Jack asked, stunned.

"According to my information, Mr. Laurence resigned today," the woman replied.

"He left the same day Hewitt died," Jack said, thinking out loud. He thanked the receptionist and hung up.

A fan of Michael Connelly, Dennis Lehane, and Elmore Leonard novels, Jack began to piece together an intricate crime thriller, with the mysterious and sinister Bob Laurence serving as the antagonist. The plot bubble burst when Jack's phone rang. It was Andy Barrows.

"Did you hear?" Barrows asked.

"Hear what?"

"The *Tribune* just posted the story. The board of directors is going to hold an emergency meeting this Friday to discuss an interim CEO. And according to this, they've got a very short list of candidates."

"Friday? Isn't that the day after Hewitt's funeral?"

"I know, bad for PR," Barrows said. "The *Trib* plays that up plenty. But it's not like they'll be holding the meeting around the man's casket, and all the board members will be in town for the service."

"Any names?"

"No names. But the stock has already taken a good hit, and they evidently don't want the good ship Hewitt and its 2.3 billion dollars in annual revenue sailing without someone at the helm for very long."

CHAPTER 3

THE COMPETITION

Wednesday crawled by. Jack did his best to remain focused on his department's latest project: improving Primo's online gaming service, Portal.

Hewitt Games had launched Portal nearly four years ago, allowing console gamers around the world to connect and compete with one another over the Web. It was by far the most popular online gaming service on the market, with more than two million paid subscribers. According to Howard Hewitt, that was all the more reason to work harder to make Portal even better.

Jack's team was following standard procedure to compile all of the data the company's creative teams and strategy gurus would require to chart the best course. Data from focus groups and customer surveys, detailed market research reports, and a complete analysis of top competitor Sampson Electronics' online product, Hive, were all being compiled.

Jack grinned. Hive couldn't touch Portal, and that was straight from the mouths of his two kids, Cody, thirteen, and Keri, eleven. What better competitor analysis was there than that?

"Got a second, boss?"

Jack looked up to see his department's newest member, Julie Sawyer, standing in the doorway to his office. Fresh out of B-school, Julie had been with Hewitt for nearly six months. She was full of energy and ideas, traits Turner knew he would have to nurture without letting the dreamer fly off track.

"Sure, Julie," Jack said. "Come on in."

"It's nothing serious, at least I don't think so, just take a minute," she said, sitting down on the edge of the armchair in front of Turner's desk. "I'm still learning the ropes, so I figured I might as well run something past you, just to be sure."

Jack smiled. "I'm intrigued."

"Well, as I told HR during the initial interviews, I'd also applied at Sampson."

"I remember," Jack said. "Always nice to know we're the top choice for top talent."

"Thanks," Sawyer said, blushing slightly. "Anyway, when I had my very first interview with the recruiter for Sampson, she made it very clear they were looking to hire someone quickly. She didn't get into any specifics, of course, but she also intimated that they were looking to hire in a number of departments."

"Well, the industry is booming," Jack said. "Last year alone, gaming took in over ten billion dollars."

"Oh, I know," she replied, looking slightly embarrassed. "It's just that … I've started helping out on our Hive analysis, and it got me thinking about Sampson and that interview I had. That's why I thought I should tell you … I came away from that initial interview thinking Sampson was starting to work on something *really* big. Probably nothing serious, like I said. I just wanted to make sure to run it by you."

"Thanks, Julie, really," Jack said. "I appreciate the fact you want to look out for Hewitt's best interests already. But I wouldn't chalk it up to anything more than the growth of the entire industry. Besides, consoles run on ten-year cycles. So we've got a good two years before the next new console war with Sampson heats up."

"That's what I figured," she said, standing to leave with a smile. "Sorry to interrupt."

"Anytime," Jack said as she walked out the door.

He turned his attention back to his monitor. After a moment, he noticed that his eyes hadn't registered anything on the screen, and something Sawyer had said was playing on a loop in his mind. A sudden realization made the thought far worse: Sampson was working on something *really* big, and Howard Hewitt was gone.

CHAPTER 4

STARVING FOR REAL INTELLIGENCE

On Thursday morning, the gothic spire of the historic Holy Name Cathedral on North State Street appeared to poke at the mass of low-hanging clouds directly overhead. Jack Turner was sure the spire would catch one, tear it open, and unleash a torrent of rain on the hundreds of mourners below.

"Whatcha looking at, hon?" Sofia asked.

"April showers," Jack replied. "Just wondering if we're going to get wet." He smiled at his wife of sixteen years and kissed her on the cheek.

"We'll be inside before long," she said, pointing to the cathedral's enormous bronze doors. "Looks like they're bringing the casket out now."

Through the arched doors the pallbearers emerged with the bullet-gray burden on their shoulders. As they passed by the lines of gathered mourners, Jack silently said his final good-bye to the man he'd admired and feared for so many years.

When the casket was lowered and pushed into the waiting hearse, one of the pallbearers caught Jack's eye. He was an older man with buzz-cut, salt-and-pepper hair and a barrel chest.

Jack leaned to his left and whispered to Barrows, "He look familiar to you?"

Barrows saw whom Jack was eyeing and replied, "That's Bob Laurence, Hewitt's sidekick."

"That's Laurence?"

"In the flesh."

"I'd been meaning to ask you about him," Jack said. "You know what he did for the company?"

"He was a senior VP, but I'm not exactly sure of what. Why? You heard the rumor about the mystery man who got rid of Hewitt so he could take over?" Barrows grinned and elbowed his friend.

"Something like that," Jack said with a smile.

"To be honest, I was never sure exactly what he did either. But when you've been with a company like Hewitt Games since the very beginning *and* you're close to the founder and CEO, you can do pretty much whatever you want."

Jack nodded. "I suppose. When you put it that way, it explains why he resigned the day Hewitt died."

"Exactly," Barrows said. "The new boss, whoever it turns out to be, inevitably would have given Laurence his walking papers. Laurence read the writing on the wall and made his exit gracefully."

The sound of the hearse's door closing drew both men's attention, and they watched in silence as the long black vehicle pulled away from the curb. As if on cue, it finally began to rain.

* * *

As a steady rain tapped at his bedroom window and his wife Sofia murmured in her sleep, Jack Turner tossed. He finally rose at 2:00 AM and checked on the kids before padding down to his study.

He logged onto Hewitt's system and started searching for everything they had on Sampson Electronics. There had to be something in this mountain of data that would indicate whether or not Hewitt's nemesis had something in the works. At least that's what Jack hoped.

He scoured the facts and figures, the projections and estimates, the insight from analysts and experts for hours, hoping to find some clue. When Sofia walked into the study at 6:00 AM, he was still searching.

"Did you catch the worm?" she asked, rubbing the sleep from her eyes.

Jack shook his head. "Guess I wasn't early enough."

Sofia tilted her head to the side and smiled. "Everything all right, hon?"

Jack sighed. "I just can't shake this feeling that everything at work is about to change, just like that—" he snapped his fingers for effect "—and there's nothing I can do about it."

Sofia walked behind his chair and wrapped her arms around his shoulders. "Howard Hewitt was bigger than life. With him suddenly gone, it's natural to feel that way."

"I know. But that's only part of it." Jack pulled a hand down over his face. "I heard a rumor that Sampson Electronics might be working on something big. It was probably nothing, but ever since I got word, it's been eating me up. And it if *is* true, if Sampson is getting a head start on the next big gaming system, how will Hewitt Games be able to respond without Howard Hewitt?"

Sofia started to offer reassurance, but Jack cut her off. "Wait, there's more. If I'm Sampson and I'm thinking, just thinking, about the possibility of an early launch for a new console, wouldn't I now push ahead full throttle with Hewitt gone and seize the opportunity? Of course I would! Hewitt's been beating me for years. This is a huge opportunity!"

Sofia could see that her husband wasn't done venting. and she waited patiently as he collected his thoughts.

"The worst part, what kept me up all night and had me on this computer at two o'clock in the morning, is this—part of my job is to see these things coming, Sofia. I'm supposed to help keep Hewitt out in front by knowing the market forward and back. And I do. My department gathers all of this information, all of this data and research to help us stay on top. But two things dawned on me as the sun was coming up, and I was searching for a needle in a haystack. First, none of this data is exclusive information our competitors don't also have access to. Second, and most important, this information may tell us everything about the market, but it tells us next to nothing about the competition. We're drowning in all of this information, yet we're starving for real intelligence."

"If that's true," Sofia said, "then how did Hewitt Games manage to top Sampson Electronics and everyone else out there for so many years?"

"It was the man himself and his drive for innovation," Jack replied. "And they laid him to rest this morning."

CHAPTER 5

SUSAN WRIGHT

The company-wide e-mail message arrived in Jack Turner's inbox late Friday afternoon. The straightforward subject line brought Jack to the edge of his chair:

BOARD OF DIRECTORS ELECTS INTERIM CEO

He clicked the message open without hesitation.

Valued Hewitt Games personnel:

Howard Hewitt made Hewitt Games the most successful video game console developer in the world by constantly pushing forward. The untimely passing of Mr. Hewitt has shaken this great company, but his philosophy remains its bedrock.

It was this philosophy that spurred the board of directors to move quickly to elect an interim CEO, because without senior leadership, this organization cannot move forward. It was a difficult decision, and the board believes it has elected the best candidate for the job, Susan Wright.

For the past five years, Ms. Wright has served as president of Hewitt Games' Handheld Division. Prior to that, Ms. Wright was the founder and CEO of HandsOn, creator of the popular GoGame handheld device. Hewitt Games acquired HandsOn in 2002, and Ms. Wright has been instrumental in merging HandsOn with Hewitt Games and generating, year over year, double-digit growth in the company's handheld division.

Ms. Wright will address the company in an all-employee conference call scheduled for 1:00 PM CST on Monday, April 21.

Jack skimmed over the rest of the message: a collection of glowing quotes from board members about Wright. Hewitt's Handheld Division was based in San Francisco, and Jack had only met Susan Wright a few times at various company functions. She was funny, bright, and personable, but one thing stood out in Jack's mind: Susan Wright was the exact opposite of Howard Hewitt.

The phone rang as Jack was reaching for it.

"Thoughts?" Andy Barrows asked.

"You first."

"It's like comparing an eighteen-wheeler and a sports car," Barrows said. "Completely different strengths and weaknesses."

"The board obviously knew that going in. Why do you think they went for such a drastic change?"

"Hewitt's tirades in board meetings are legendary. I'm guessing that influenced their decision just a tad."

"True. I can't imagine Susan Wright throwing an executive's chair across the boardroom. The question is, will a different chief executive with a vastly different management style want to put different people in leadership roles?"

"It crossed my mind," Barrows said. "There's no doubt we'll have to prove ourselves a bit to Wright. But we had to prove our worth to Howard Hewitt every minute of every day, so this should be a breeze."

"I've got to run," Jack said. "The troops are getting restless."

"And I'm already getting e-mail about coordinating with Wright's people," Barrows replied. "Talk to you soon."

Jack hung up and heard the chatter in the department rising. He walked out among the cubicles and felt a nervous tension in the air.

"All right, everyone," he said, raising his voice. "We've just received some big news. Big news indeed."

Those who weren't already on their feet stood to see their boss.

"And we've already had plenty of news to deal with this week," Jack continued. "Why doesn't everyone take a fifteen-minute break, get some of the jitters out, and then we'll come back and get to work. Remember what the message from the board said—this company made it to the top by constantly pushing forward. I'd like to think this department is a big part of that forward progress, and we've got an important project to work on. As you all know, that project comes with a deadline. Let's not forget that. The last thing we want to do with a new CEO coming on board is miss a deadline. In spite of all the shocking news, we've done a bang-up job this week. Let's keep it up."

Jack's mini-pep talk drew nods and smiles—a good sign any potential fires had been extinguished. As team members made their way out of the office, Jack noticed Julie Sawyer and thought there was one more fire he should try to contain—at least for now.

"Julie, can I speak with you for a second?"

"Sure, what's up?"

Jack waited for the department's other employees to file out, and then he nodded for Julie to follow at the tail end of the pack and out of earshot.

"The other day you mentioned your experience with the Sampson recruiter," Jack began.

"Something come up?" Julie asked, eyes wide.

"No, nothing like that. Everything is fine. I just wanted to make sure you knew everything was okay. And I wanted to ask you to keep what we discussed private. Did you mention it to anyone else, your thoughts about Sampson?"

"No, no one," Julie said, shaking her head.

"Good. I know I can trust you. Everyone has had plenty to ponder this week," Jack said, thinking about his own sleepless nights. "I would hate to add something like that to the list."

"I completely understand, and you can completely trust me. I'll keep my crazy theories to myself," she said with a laugh.

Jack thanked Julie and watched her catch up with her co-workers. He couldn't help but think, *It's not nearly as crazy as you think.*

CHAPTER 6

JOB DESCRIPTION

Despite Old Man Winter's best efforts to prolong a particularly miserable season with an early April snowstorm, spring was now in full bloom in Chicago.

Jack Turner felt rejuvenated by the bright sunshine and clear blue skies that greeted him on his morning run, and the sixty-degree weather felt almost tropical.

Change is good, Jack reassured himself as his running shoes pounded the pavement. *And if there's a crisis, so be it. In crisis comes opportunity.*

When he finished his five-mile loop, he found his two kids playing catch on the front lawn and his wife planting flowers in the garden. Seeing Sofia, Cody, and Keri enjoying the weather in front of the home he'd worked so hard for, Jack made a spur-of-the-moment decision: this would be a family weekend. There would be no work, or even thoughts of Hewitt Games, for two days. While his intentions were altruistic, Jack also knew that starting Monday, his job could very well become all-consuming.

And so it was.

Jack managed to finagle a deal for Hewitt's box at Wrigley Field for Saturday afternoon's Cubs game, and the kids went bonkers. That evening, Jack and Sofia dropped Keri and Cody off at the Barrows' household for the night and made it to Sofia's favorite restaurant, Tru, for a late dinner.

"I love you, Jack, and I love what you did for the kids and me today," Sofia said as they lay in bed at the end of a long day. "But I also know how you work. So tell me honestly, how bad is it going to be?"

Jack kissed his wife. "I'll have a better idea after Wright addresses the company on Monday, but there's no doubt I'm going to be in hustle mode for a few months, especially if Sampson starts to make a move."

Sofia nodded and draped an arm across her husband's chest. "Be sure to let the kids know," she said.

"I promise," Jack said. "And I plan on running them ragged with activities tomorrow. They'll be so sick of dear old Dad by tomorrow night, they'll be avoiding me like the plague for the next three months."

* * *

Jack Turner saw every minute of the morning tick by on Monday. As much as he tried to focus on his work, he couldn't stop his eyes from drifting to his watch, or to the digital clocks on his computer monitor, desk phone, and cell phone.

Andy Barrows called every hour on the hour, trying to ease the anticipation of Susan Wright's all-employee conference call with his trademark humor. And when the phone rang just before noon, Jack couldn't help but assume it was his friend.

"You're like a teenage girl with this thing, you know that?" Jack said with a laugh.

"I've been called many things in my sixty-two years," came the gravelly voice on the other end. "But that is the first time *anyone* has ever compared me to a teenage girl."

Jack's eyes went wide. "Oh, God, I'm so sorry! I thought it was someone else. This is a red-faced Jack Turner. Can I help you?"

"Jack, this is Bob Laurence. I recently resigned from Hewitt. Perhaps you remember speaking with me in the past?"

"Mr. Laurence, of course I remember. I apologize."

"Good. I'll make this quick, Jack. When I retired on Tuesday, the day Howard died, stock in Hewitt Games was near its all-time high. If there was any time for me to walk away, it was on Tuesday. I just checked the ticker, and I see we're nearly all the way down to Sampson's level. The board was wise to make a quick move in naming an interim CEO, but I'll be frank and tell you I don't think they picked the right person for the position. No offense to Ms. Wright—she's a fine executive. And it has nothing to do with her gender. The bottom line is that Hewitt Games demands a leader, not a consensus builder. It's obvious Wall Street feels the same way."

"Well, I—"

"Let me ask you something, Jack. What do you think is going on over at Sampson Electronics right now?"

Jack swallowed hard. Laurence took it as a response.

"I'll tell you what's going on. They're having a party. 'Howard Hewitt's gone!' That's what they're cheering. 'We can finally beat Hewitt!'"

Jack experienced déjà vu—he felt like he was having a conversation with Howard Hewitt himself. Unconsciously, he slipped into shut-up-and-listen mode.

"Let me tell you something, Jack. That ain't gonna happen. It only happened once in twenty-five years on my watch, and I swore to Howard it would never happen again. But because I'm no longer with the company, and because there's no chance anyone else at the company would listen to what I have to say or do the hard work that needs to be done, I'm going to need your help."

"M-my help?" Jack stammered.

"Meet me for lunch tomorrow afternoon, and I'll give you all the details. Got a pen?"

Jack scrambled for pen and paper and scribbled out the time and address as Laurence shot it out in rapid fire.

"Wait, Mr. Laurence," Jack said before Laurence could hang up. "I just wanted to know … what exactly is it that you did at Hewitt?"

"Simple," Laurence replied, "I made sure the roof was repaired while the sun was shining."

CHAPTER 7

NEW DIRECTION

"I am not Howard Hewitt," Susan Wright began, her soft voice clear on the conference call. "Nor will I try to be."

Jack sat in the conference room with his team, all twenty people gathered around the speakerphone. Everyone stared intently at the device as if they could see the words it emitted.

"There is no other Howard Hewitt, and there never will be. We all know it was his presence, and his style of over-the-shoulder management, that kept Hewitt Games flying high. The question is, how do we make sure the company doesn't crash, now that Mr. Hewitt is gone?"

Here Wright paused. Jack wasn't sure if it was for dramatic effect or if she had lost her place, but the new CEO's last words had raised the tension level in the room considerably.

"The answer is simple—we all have to work together. We can no longer work in the disciplined silos that Mr. Hewitt created. We have to come together in all departments and begin working as a cross-functional team. We will have to communicate, from the top to the bottom and from the bottom to the top, like we never have before. 'Open' is the operative term here. We must all work together as one organization to set goals, and everyone must know what their individual and departmental responsibilities are as we work to achieve those goals."

Wright continued to describe the culture change that had to transpire at Hewitt Games and concluded her speech on an upbeat note.

"Perhaps Howard Hewitt's greatest and least talked about accomplishment was in recruiting and hiring all of you. Few could argue that he hadn't assembled the most talented and dedicated team in the industry. It is because of this, because of all of you, that Hewitt Games will not only survive without its iconic founder, it will rise to even greater heights. I look forward to the ride, and I hope you do too."

The call ended, and after a brief moment of silence filled with smiles and nodding heads, everyone burst into applause. Jack joined in, but without the same level of enthusiasm as his team members. He was still thinking about Bob Laurence's cryptic last words about roof repair.

* * *

Jack's stomach rumbled. He looked at his watch and saw that somehow it was 7:35 PM.

"Damn," Jack said, picking up his cell phone. He'd told Sofia he'd be home by 7:30.

"Honey, sorry, I lost track of time. I'm leaving now. Be home in twenty minutes."

Jack hit the department's main lights on his way out and stopped short when he heard a voice. He flipped the lights back on and saw Julie Sawyer stand up at her cubicle.

"Sorry about that, Julie," Jack said, looking at his watch. "Just assumed I was the last one here."

"No problem, boss," Julie replied. "I thought I was the last one here too."

"What's keeping you so late?"

"Just trying to get ahead. You?"

"Susan Wright is going to be in the office tomorrow, and she's scheduled meetings with all the department heads. I wanted to make sure I was prepared."

"Anything I can do to help?" Julie offered.

Jack smiled. "No, thank you. I'll be fine. But I appreciate it, Julie, really. And thank you for all your hard work. It hasn't gone unnoticed. Don't stay too late."

Jack said good-bye and made his way to the elevator. As he descended to the parking garage, he remembered his first interview with Julie Sawyer. When asked to describe her strongest trait, Sawyer had replied, "Never saying, 'That's not my job.'"

To Jack, it initially sounded like a clever spin on "my work ethic," but Sawyer hadn't hesitated to offer a more detailed response.

"My family is in the restaurant business. My dad runs the bar, my mom runs the kitchen, and my uncle manages the dining room. A real family affair. I started helping out as soon as my parents gave me the okay. They threw everything at me over the years—prep cooking, washing dishes, working the line, hostessing, bar-backing, waiting tables, you name it.

"By the time I was in high school, there was a good chance I was doing a little bit of all of those things on any given night. If the kitchen was getting slammed while I was hostessing, I wasn't afraid to throw on an apron and get on the line for a few minutes. It's the type of do-whatever-it-takes mentality my parents not only expected, they demanded. And it taught me an important lesson—real success happens in any business when you have a group of people who would never dream of saying, 'Sorry, that's not my job.'"

The elevator opened to the parking garage, and Jack stepped out. He had a feeling Susan Wright would expect much the same mentality from all of Hewitt's employees, and he was glad to have someone like Julie Sawyer on board.

CHAPTER 8

CLOAK AND DAGGER

Hackney's, down on Printer's Row, was old-school Chicago, and it buzzed with lunchtime activity. Jack Turner followed the maitre d' to the back of the bustling dining room and a corner table where Bob Laurence sat alone.

"Afternoon, Mr. Laurence," Jack said, extending a slightly sweaty hand.

Laurence pulled his nose from the pages of *The Wall Street Journal* and removed a pair of thick glasses.

"There you are," Laurence said, standing to accept the greeting. He checked his watch. "I was afraid you weren't going to show."

"Traffic," Jack said. "Sorry I'm running late."

"That's all right," Laurence replied. "Sit down. Are you hungry? Like something to drink?"

"Afraid I don't have much time," Jack said, waving off the waiter as both men sat. "Susan Wright is in the office today, and I'm scheduled to meet with her a little after lunch."

"Meet the new boss," Laurence said with a nod. "Then let's get right to it." The old man took a deep breath and exhaled. He looked Jack square in the eye. "Yesterday, you asked me what I did at Hewitt Games. Do you remember what I said?"

Jack smiled nervously. He'd been thinking about Laurence's words since they last spoke. "You said you made sure the roof was repaired while the sun was shining. Probably the most unusual job description I've ever heard."

Jack laughed. Laurence did not.

"It's a take on a JFK quote. It means I was proactive worldwide in making sure Hewitt Games was always ready for stormy weather. If you're reactive and only fix the roof when it starts to leak, you get all wet."

"I get the gist of it," Jack said, clearing his throat. "But I still don't know what that means in terms of your job, your everyday responsibilities at the company."

"Allow me to explain," Laurence said. "You might recall, back in the late 1980s, Hewitt's console ruled the world."

Jack nodded. He knew the story as well as anyone at Hewitt Games. Throughout the 1980s, Hewitt's Primo commanded an untouchable 90 percent of the market, while a handful of competitors fought over the remaining scraps.

Laurence continued, "You might also recall that in 1989, Hewitt Games was seemingly blindsided by Sampson's first console."

Jack shrugged. "It's fairly common knowledge. Hewitt Games saw its market share shrink from 90 percent to 60 percent almost overnight when Sampson was the first to launch a sixteen-bit console, double the processing power of the eight-bit Primo. A short time later, Hewitt Games briefly fell into second place in the industry for the first and only time in its history."

"That's right," Laurence said, leaning forward. "We were more than six months behind Sampson in releasing our own sixteen-bit machine. Not because we didn't have the talent, or the investment in R&D. We had plans for a sixteen-bit console as early as 1986!" The old man slapped the table and rattled the silverware. "We easily could have released a new machine before Sampson did."

Jack swallowed before asking, "So why didn't you?"

Laurence wagged a finger. "That's what everyone wanted to know," he said, nodding repeatedly. "We were on top, we were the innovators. How could we let a rinky-dink startup beat us at our own game? How could we let the competition win? The answer is simple, Jack—we just didn't know. In the words of John Conway, 'The two most common reasons for losing are not knowing you're competing in the first place, and not knowing with whom you're competing.' Sure, we got wind that Sampson was working on a new box, but the fact is, we knew nothing about that company. And we didn't do anything to learn about them or what they were actually trying to do. We thought we were the masters of the universe. Sampson proved us wrong. There was a gaping hole in our roof, and we got all wet."

"But you obviously learned from your mistake," Jack said. "Hewitt Games was rattled, but it managed to get back on top, and that's exactly where we are today."

"You've hit the nail right on the head," Laurence said, sliding up to the edge of his seat. "We did learn from our mistake. On the day Sampson launched its sixteen-bit machine, we promised we would never take the competition for granted again. We made absolutely sure we knew everything we could about what was going on at that company and how it would impact our business. That was my job, Jack. That was my everyday responsibility at Hewitt Games—to find out what the competition was up to and gather the information we needed to make damn well sure we stayed one step ahead."

Jack's stomach suddenly felt hollow. He leaned back in his seat and felt the blood rush into his face. "And just how exactly did you go about doing that, Mr. Laurence?"

Laurence leaned in even closer and lowered his voice to a volume just above a whisper. "Are you familiar with competitive intelligence?"

Jack nearly swooned. The pieces of the puzzle abruptly slammed into place, creating a disturbing image. Bob Laurence, the mystery man at Hewitt Games, Howard Hewitt's right hand, the man who conveniently resigned the day the founder died, was the company spook. Everything Jack thought he knew about Hewitt Games and its iconic founder immediately flew out the window.

Jack's voice cracked. "That's why you tell people your job was fixing roofs? Because you were some kind of corporate espionage expert?"

Heads turned at nearby tables.

Laurence's face went white. "Wait, Jack, I don't know what you've heard, but—"

"Save it," Jack said, bolting upright. "I don't want to hear any more, not a single word about your cloak-and-dagger heroics. And I certainly don't want to become a part of them."

27

"This is what Howard was afraid of," Laurence said, shaking his head and standing as Jack turned away. "Please, Jack, you've got to listen to me. The company needs competitive intelligence now more than ever."

Power lunches stopped in mid-chew as Jack pushed his way through the dining room and Bob Laurence called out after him, "Jack, please!"

CHAPTER 9

THE FORTY-SECOND

Andy Barrows looked at Jack Turner with wide eyes. He stood and began pacing behind his desk, his hands behind his back like a captain on the quarterdeck. For the first time Jack could recall, Barrows was speechless.

"You remember when we were ramping up the last Primo system?" Jack asked.

Barrows nodded but remained silent.

"We'd been working around the clock for a year to ensure a holiday launch. Everything was set, all our hard work had paid off, and then out of nowhere Hewitt slammed on the brakes at the last minute. He said we absolutely had to have the online component of the system complete. We'd originally planned on making Portal an add-on. But Hewitt himself said it was Portal that would put the system over the top. And guess what? He was dead on. We launched two months behind Sampson's new machine, after the holiday season, but it didn't matter. Sampson didn't offer online play. Portal was the thing that put us over the top, and Sampson is still playing catch-up."

Barrows stopped in his tracks. "Hewitt knew."

Jack nodded. "He knew because he had his man Laurence doing God knows what to steal information from Sampson."

Barrows slumped back down into his chair. "All those strokes of genius Hewitt was famous for, all those hunches about strategy ..."

"Not hunches," Jack said. "Decisions based on information gathered in a manner that probably wasn't legal and couldn't possibly be ethical."

"Talk about playing with a stacked deck. We all knew how competitive Hewitt was, but this? The image I had of that man ... I feel like a kid who just learned there's no such thing as Santa Claus."

"I know," Jack said. "Hard to believe."

Both men let their own thoughts simmer.

"You're meeting with Wright in what—twenty minutes?" Barrows finally asked, glancing at his watch. "Will you tell her?"

"No," Jack said, shaking his head. "Hewitt is gone, and Laurence is retired. As far as I'm concerned, whatever they did is in the past. It's time to start working on the future of this company."

* * *

The elevator chimed, and its doors slid open on the forty-second floor. The *Forty-Second*, Jack thought, the simple name carrying with it a ton of emotion. Being called up to Howard Hewitt's lair was enough to make even an atheist utter a prayer.

But this was no longer the Forty-Second; Jack could feel it the moment he stepped off of the elevator. He was nervous about officially meeting the new boss, sure, but the sensation was nothing like the panic-inducing anticipation of seeing the old boss. Jack felt even more at ease when he saw his friend and colleague, Anna Patel, Hewitt's CMO. She emerged from the CEO's office with a smile on her face.

"Hey, Anna," Jack said. "I'd ask you how it went in there, but you're grinning like the Cheshire cat."

"You'll soon see why," she said, patting Jack on the shoulder as she walked by.

Jack checked in with Susan Wright's assistant and took a seat. A moment later he was ushered into the chief executive's office.

The view was just as Jack remembered it: breathtaking. The spacious corner office provided a postcard-perfect view of the city.

"Jack, hi," Susan Wright said, rounding a long mahogany desk with her hand extended.

"Great to see you, Susan," Jack said, shaking her hand. "Congratulations."

"Thank you. Unexpected, to be sure. And I wish it had happened under different circumstances. It's been a whirlwind few days." She shook her head and smiled. "Have a seat, and let's chat."

Wright led the way to a set of comfortable leather armchairs positioned around a glass coffee table. After a few moments of small talk, the chief executive began the formal discussion by telling Jack she had meant what she'd said in her company-wide address.

"My job will be to help set the strategy and make sure you, and all the other department heads, have the tools you need to get the job done," she said. "After that, it will be in your hands. You don't need me to tell you how to do your job. I have complete trust in all of our talented people."

"That's refreshing to hear," Jack said. "I have no doubt we'll rise to the challenge."

"Good," Wright said, "because I have no doubt either, particularly when it comes to market research. I've been going over your department's performance over the past few years, Jack. Your contributions have been invaluable. We've been able to beat Sampson to the punch time after time, and I know that wouldn't have been possible without your department providing the best market research and analysis in the industry."

Jack felt the blood rush into his face. An image of Bob Laurence popped into his head, leaning in close and asking in his sand-and-gravel voice, "Are you familiar with competitive intelligence?"

"Thank you for the compliment," Jack said. "But I have to give credit where it's due. Howard Hewitt was a visionary."

Wright waved a hand at Jack. "You're too modest. No matter how big the Hewitt legend is, I know he wouldn't have been able to make those decisions without your critical input. The point is, we're going to need your department's expertise more than ever over the next six months. We'll be making some very big decisions about the future of this company, and we've got to have the very best information available to make sure we don't stray down the wrong path. Sampson is just waiting for us to slip up. You'll play a leading role in making sure that doesn't happen."

Jack swallowed. "Of course."

"Terrific," Wright said, rising from her seat. "Thanks for coming up today, Jack. We'll have plenty to discuss very soon."

Jack's head was swimming. He had no idea what he said to Wright in parting; the words just fell from his mouth. He pasted a fake smile on his face, waved good-bye to Wright's assistant, and tried not to run through the waiting room. When the elevator doors finally, mercifully slid closed, he slumped against the wall.

"Now what?"

CHAPTER 10

JUNE 23

After commiserating with Andy Barrows, Jack Turner returned to his office and closed the door. He felt as if he'd unknowingly fallen down the rabbit hole, into another world where everything he knew was turned upside down and inside out.

The worst part was that Jack had no idea how to escape from Wonderland. Sampson Electronics was no doubt plotting the demise of Hewitt Games, and Jack felt absolutely powerless to stop it. How could he? Without Bob Laurence playing 007, Hewitt Games knew as much about the competition as industry reports and analysis revealed—information available to anyone.

And when Sampson did make its inevitable move, Jack knew he would end up facing Susan Wright on the Forty-Second.

Jack picked up the phone and called his wife, hoping Sofia's soothing voice would help calm his rattled nerves. He'd originally planned to simply check in on her day, but his own story came pouring out the moment she asked, "How is your day going?"

From his illuminating lunch with Laurence to his meeting with Wright where the bar was set at an unimaginable height, Jack told Sofia everything.

"I'm giving new meaning to the phrase 'stuck between a rock and a hard place,'" he said.

"Is it really that bad?" Sofia asked.

"It wouldn't be if Wright didn't think I had some sort of crystal ball. But evidently she does, so the expectations are completely off the charts."

"You can't tell her what was going on, what this Laurence guy was doing?"

"I'm afraid it would put a black mark on everyone," Jack said. "The 'I didn't know' excuse isn't much of a shield. And besides, what do I tell her? I'm not even sure exactly *what* Laurence was doing."

"Well, maybe it wasn't as terrible as you think."

"Maybe, but there must have been a reason why Hewitt kept such a tight lid on it. No one in this company knew what Laurence did, not even Andy, and he's the head of human resources!"

"That *is* suspicious," Sofia said. "I'm sorry you've had such a tough week, hon. Just remember, you're the one that always says that in crisis comes opportunity. This qualifies as a crisis, so where is the opportunity?"

"If there is an opportunity," Jack said with a sigh, "I just don't see it."

After the conversation with his wife, Jack did feel a bit relieved—at least enough to get some work done. He clicked his computer out of sleep mode and opened his e-mail. The messages had piled up since he last checked his inbox before leaving for lunch.

Jack made his way through the long list, sending replies, making phone calls, and jotting down notes. The typically tedious work was now a welcome distraction, taking Jack's mind off of his predicament until he clicked on an urgent message with the subject line *JUNE 23.*

Jack didn't recognize the sender, and the date didn't ring a bell. His first thought was that one of Sofia's recently engaged friends was announcing a wedding date.

Jack:

I understand your trepidation. Unfortunately, even companies that embrace competitive intelligence, like Hewitt Games, tend to keep it quiet. Perhaps after June 23 you will begin to understand how important competitive intelligence is to this company's success. I await your call.

—Bob Laurence

Jack read the message again before looking at his calendar. Nothing stood out. It was now the middle of May. As far as he could tell, Hewitt Games had nothing planned for June 23.

Jack's heart skipped a beat when it dawned on him that Laurence wasn't talking about Hewitt. He entered the date on his calendar. Jack counted the days and thought with dread, *What does Sampson have planned for June 23?*

CHAPTER 11

BE PREPARED

The alarm sounded at 5:00 AM, stirring Jack Turner from a restless sleep. A dream sank into the depths of his subconscious before his waking mind could reel it back in.

It had been like this for the past two weeks. Jack struggled to fall asleep at night, and fitful dreams he could never quite remember filled his slumber.

Bleary-eyed, Jack showered, shaved, and got dressed. He was out the door by 5:30 AM, and he made it to Hewitt Games just before 6:00.

Alone in the office, Jack checked various media outlets for the day's business news, hunting for a headline about Sampson Electronics. When he found nothing on the competition, he was not relieved. He looked at his calendar and hoped Sampson would do something, anything, before June 23.

Sitting in his office, alone and tired, Jack focused his thoughts on June 23. And suddenly, inexplicably, he saw the opportunity. It was as if he'd finally hooked the dream that had eluded him for the past two weeks. Sampson would throw a punch on June 23—of that, Jack had little doubt. Hewitt Games would not be able to stop it. What the company *could* do, however, was to load up with a counterpunch of its own.

* * *

"Portal," Jack said. "Our online service is the reason why our latest console beat Sampson's, and it's the best tool we can use to counter anything they throw at us in the short term."

Susan Wright and the other executives seated around the conference table looked on in silence. Jack still felt stunned to find himself standing before them. His urgent e-mail to Wright that morning had not only been heard but also acted upon with surprising speed.

"We've done the legwork to find out how best to improve Portal, and our designers and programmers are already working on the update. What we need now is to get it done as quickly as possible."

Susan Wright turned to address Hewitt's COO, Peter Allen. "Pete, when was the Primo update scheduled for release?"

"The weekend of July 26," Allen replied.

"Reassign anyone not working on Portal who can help us move that date up dramatically. Find out what those people need to get the job done, and give it to them."

Wright turned next to the chief marketing officer, Anna Patel. "We've got to package the Portal update with offers gamers can't refuse."

Patel adjusted her reading glasses. "We can make a popular online title free with the purchase of a new Primo, combine that with a month of access to Portal at no charge."

"Good," Wright said, jotting down notes. "And let's not forget about our current Portal subscribers. Let's reward them for being loyal customers."

"Will do," Patel said with a nod.

Wright continued around the table, giving assignments and receiving input from each senior executive. She finished with Jack.

"We'll need your input on how to best tweak this package to have the biggest impact with consumers," she said.

"On it," Jack replied.

Wright stood. "All right, everyone, we knew Sampson would make a move—it was just a matter of when. I know we'd normally have a healthy internal discussion about all of this before making any rapid shifts, but because I trust what Jack is saying, I have to make an executive decision. We don't have time to debate the rationale and wait for everyone involved to buy into this shift in priorities and resources. Let's do everything we can to make sure we're ready to respond."

As the executive team filed out of the conference room, Wright asked Jack to stay. When everyone else had left, she pointed to a nearby seat.

"Your track record speaks for itself, Jack. That's why I didn't hesitate to act on this. But this wasn't the type of information I anticipated you providing."

Jack knew the question before Wright asked it: "How exactly did you find out about Sampson's plans for June 23?"

Even though Jack knew the question was coming, he still wasn't sure how best to respond. He couldn't tell an outright lie; it just wasn't in his nature to do so. But he also couldn't tell Wright the complete story, in part because he didn't know the complete story himself.

"We hear things in my department, doing the work we do. Snippets of information about this and that. We got wind of something big happening on June 23 … and I made the connection to Sampson."

"That's it?" Wright asked with a raised brow. "You heard something? Nothing more specific?"

Jack felt his temperature rising. "Nothing specific, just the date. But like you said, we knew Sampson was going to make a move. Even if it turns out not to be June 23, it won't be long after. I thought it was critical to get us prepared to respond."

Wright looked away for a moment, the exasperation clear on her face. "Jack, you may have a point there, but I've got to tell you, I'm shocked. You can't expect this company to act based on vague or anecdotal information and gut feelings."

"Absolutely not," Jack said, holding up his hands. "Please believe me—that's not what I do, not what my department does. I never would have brought something like this to your attention if not for the … unique circumstances."

Wright looked at Jack with cool blue eyes. "I've been preaching trust since day one. I'd be a hypocrite if I didn't trust you now. But let me also make something abundantly clear. One side of my coin reads trust—the other side reads accountability. The next time you hit the panic button, you damn well better have a whole lot more than a date and a hunch. Because trust me, if you don't, I will hold you accountable."

CHAPTER 12

REELHD

Susan Wright had talked about tearing down the silos and creating an environment of teamwork and open communication. In the weeks leading up to June 23, she began to do just that.

Wright clearly communicated the organization's goal to all departments and got everyone behind the Portal project with an energy and enthusiasm that was contagious.

"She's walking the walk," Andy Barrows said to Jack Turner. "And more importantly, people are following her lead. I'm already hearing it from a few managers—they're buying into the team concept."

Jack nodded. "If we can pull this off and respond to whatever it is Sampson has planned within a week after June 23, she'll have an early win to build off of. If Wright gets that, she'll have the entire company buying in."

"Just think, it might all be thanks to Bob Laurence," Barrows said with a grin.

Jack smiled. "You do love to push my buttons, don't you?"

"It is a hobby of mine, and I've been doing it since college—why stop now? Will you call him?"

"I don't know," Jack said. "He could be helping us, but at what risk? I just think we're better off not knowing how he found out about it." He paused for a moment and then shrugged. "But who knows? What if the old man was just trying to get me riled up for walking out on him? What if nothing happens on June 23?"

"I hate to keep pushing your buttons," Barrows replied, "but my money is on something happening—a big something."

"I know," Jack said with a sigh. "Mine too."

* * *

On Monday morning, June 23, Jack Turner finally discovered what the red circle on his wall calendar was all about: Sampson Electronics was bringing high-definition movies to the console.

The press release was on the wire at 8:00 AM sharp. It detailed Sampson's newest device and the company's latest strategy. Jack's nail-biting first thought was that the competition had just hit a home run.

With Sampson's ReelHD, a piece of hardware the size of a small CD carrying case, consumers could transform their gaming consoles into high-definition movie players at a fraction of the cost of stand-alone high-def devices. The introductory price point for ReelHD was $99.99, compared to anywhere from $250 to $500 and up for a stand-alone HD player. The ingenious little device used the existing hardware, software, and power source of Sampson's console, and it could be controlled using the company's standard wireless gaming controllers.

Sampson promised that ReelHD would be compatible with any of its future consoles, meaning consumers didn't have to worry about replacing two devices when the next-generation console was released, and it included a fifteen-dollar coupon for the popular movie rental powerhouse Double Feature. The first boxes were set to ship in a week.

Jack made an initial damage assessment of "severe." He flashed back to when his department's newest employee, Julie Sawyer, walked into his office in April and told him Sampson was working on something *really big*. Here it was, and Jack knew that Hewitt's response wasn't nearly strong enough.

Susan Wright and the rest of the executive team agreed with that assessment at an emergency meeting just two hours later.

"Given the time frame, our options, and circumstances beyond our control, focusing on the Portal update was the right move," Wright said. "And I'm proud of everyone for the work we did over the past month to bump up our release date to June 27. We may not have the wow factor of a ReelHD, but we're leveraging a strength with this Portal update."

She drank some water before continuing. "And now we have a problem. Sampson Electronics is giving our target consumers something we know they want and something that we're not offering. That is not acceptable. We need to learn everything there is to know about this new device—how it works, how it was built, what consumers think of it, the full laundry list. I want full reports from everyone by this time next week. It's time to work the problem."

Jack got more bad news when he returned to his desk: early trading on Wall Street had Sampson's stock surging on news of ReelHD. Based on share value, Hewitt Games was now locked in a virtual dead heat with its arch-nemesis and in danger of falling to second place in the industry for the first time in nearly twenty years.

Jack picked up the phone. He put it back on the receiver before picking it up again. Like it or not, it was time to call Bob Laurence.

PART 2

THE CI BIBLE: A MASTER GUIDEBOOK

CHAPTER 13

LUNCH, TAKE TWO

Bob Laurence sat at the same table in the same restaurant that Jack Turner had stormed out of a month earlier. And just as before, Laurence had his head buried in *The Wall Street Journal*.

Jack felt relieved when the old man broke the feeling of déjà vu with a different greeting: "You're not going to run out on me again, are you, Jack?"

"As long as you promise not to speak in riddles." Jack slumped into his seat, the weight of yesterday's news from Sampson still heavy on his shoulders.

"Deal," Laurence said, removing his reading glasses and folding the newspaper. "I can see how you're taking it, but how did Wright react?"

"Well, thanks to you, we knew something was coming, so she wasn't shocked. But it's safe to say she and everyone else at the company was surprised by Sampson's announcement."

"ReelHD," Laurence said with a nod. "Clever move by Sampson. Both companies have been trying to transform consoles into multimedia centers for years. It looks like they might actually succeed at doing it."

"*Might* being the hopeful term," Jack said. "ReelHD is a home run, no doubt about it."

"There are no certainties in business, especially one as competitive as ours." Laurence leaned over the table. "Please tell me you prepared some sort of response."

Jack sighed. "We did. We managed to bump up the Portal update by nearly a full month, and we're packaging some strong incentives around the release."

"That's good," Laurence said, smiling for the first time Jack could recall. "Very good. Why the disappointment? The Portal update was the right move."

Jack shrugged. "It just seems so insignificant in response to ReelHD."

"We'll see," Laurence said. "Sampson put everything they had behind the project the moment Howard died. They wanted to make a statement, and they did. But in their haste, they were bound to make mistakes with ReelHD, and inevitably it will be consumers who find them."

Jack sat back; a considerable amount of weight suddenly lifted from his shoulders. He started to speak but stopped himself. After a pause, he asked, "So, do I want to know how you came across that obviously very secret information about June 23?"

"Correction," Laurence said. "When secrets trickle down through the supply chain, they're no longer secrets—they're pieces of information. Gather up enough of them, and you can put together an interesting picture. To answer your question— isn't that why you're here today, to learn how?"

"I'm not sure," Jack said, folding his arms across his chest. "I'll listen to what you have to say, but that in no way means I condone your actions or that I will have anything to do with whatever it is that you want to do."

"Competitive intelligence," Laurence said, looking slightly amused.

Jack unfolded his arms. "That, yes. Competitive intelligence, corporate espionage, whatever you want to call it."

Laurence held up a finger. He picked up a briefcase and popped it open on the table. He removed a small black book, what looked like a ledger, and held it out to Jack.

"What's this?"

"It's your CI bible," Laurence said. "I had it printed up last week. I want you to open to the first page and read it out loud."

Jack looked at Laurence with a furrowed brow before taking the book. On the first page, he found a brief passage and read it aloud:

"Competitive Intelligence: A legal and ethical business decision support service that has grown in part out of Professor Michael Porter's scholarship at Harvard Business School. His work was first presented over thirty years ago in the thought-leading book *Competitive Strategy*."

Laurence gave a solemn nod.

Jack closed the book and set it on the table. "No offense, Mr. Laurence, but if that's what competitive intelligence really is, then why was your role with the company kept secret all these years? If it's legal and ethical, what's the problem?"

Laurence cleared his throat. "Remember how you reacted in this very restaurant when I simply mentioned the words 'competitive intelligence'?"

"To say I fled would be an accurate description."

"And that's why it was kept a secret, why Howard Hewitt didn't want the word to get out. Hewitt Games has relied heavily on competitive intelligence for nearly twenty years. Howard never would have had anything to do with it if it weren't 100 percent legal and ethical. You do believe that, don't you, Jack?"

"I want to," Jack said. He saw the look of frustration in Laurence's eyes and couldn't help but feel sorry for the old man. "I want to believe you, Mr. Laurence. I really do. But it will take more than a nice definition and an academic reference to convince me you're able to obtain this type of information about the competition without breaking the rules."

Laurence held up his hands. "I understand completely. If you'll allow me, I'll provide you with as many detailed examples as it takes to prove to you that competitive intelligence is not only legal and ethical, it's essential for sound decision making at the corporate level."

Jack took in a deep breath through his nose and let it out slowly through his mouth. "All right, Mr. Laurence. I'll listen to what you have to say. I owe you that much. Where do we begin?"

"First things first, Jack," Laurence said with a smile. The stocky old man stood and extended a thick hand. "Call me Bob."

CHAPTER 14

THE RUNDOWN ON CI

Bob Laurence insisted on buying lunch and sharing his professional history with Jack Turner before delving further into the depths of competitive intelligence.

Jack was astonished to learn that the old man was once an investigative journalist for the *Sun-Times.* Over oysters, Laurence described his past life as a writer and his fateful meeting with Howard Hewitt.

"A small Chicago start-up by the name of Hewitt Games was drawing interest from some of the city's biggest venture capital firms. Hewitt stonewalled one of our writers and made some not-too-kind remarks about the paper. Classic Howard. My editor didn't appreciate the insult, so he sent me out to find out about Hewitt Games through back channels."

Laurence shucked an oyster and grinned. "I was good at my job. Found out everything there was to know about Hewitt Games and Howard Hewitt without ever speaking to the man himself. Naturally, I gave him one last opportunity to comment. Howard's first words to me, which I shall remember until my dying day, were, 'I look forward to using your newspaper as fish wrap.'"

Jack laughed, hearing Howard Hewitt's booming voice say the line clearly in his mind.

"We published the story the next day," Laurence continued. "I got a call first thing in the morning from Howard. He hooted and hollered about us publishing private information, let me know I would be hearing from his lawyers, and then he asked me if I wanted a job."

Both men laughed. "Must have been a great article," Jack said. "He offered you a job doing what?"

"Marketing, corporate communications, public relations. Howard wanted me behind any and all information released by

Hewitt Games. He offered a starting salary that put my journalist's paycheck to shame, and I gave the *Times* my resignation that very day, August 14, 1979."

"Wow," Jack said. "Right before Hewitt Games released the first Primo and took over the gaming world."

Laurence grinned. "You know what they say about timing. When I started, we were in an office the size of a closet on the South Side, couldn't have had more than twenty people with the company at that point. A year later we were on our way uptown to an office that would accommodate more than two hundred."

"Quite a story," Jack said. "So how did you end up pulling competitive intelligence duty?"

"By the time 1989 rolled around, Hewitt Games had a 90 percent market share, I was the vice president of marketing and communications, and Howard and I had become best friends."

"And then Sampson released the first sixteen-bit console," Jack interjected.

"Exactly," Laurence said with a shake of his head. "We talked about this the last time we met. Sampson blindsided us with a superior product, and we were left wondering how it happened and how we could make sure it never happened again. Howard and I looked high and low for a solution until we came across Michael Porter's work on competitive strategy … the Harvard Business School professor you read about on the first page of the CI bible. It was brilliant stuff, decades ahead of its time."

"And that's it? Porter's work tells you how to create a competitive intelligence function?"

"No. Porter's work was the foundation. From that foundation, business leaders across the nation built what would become known as competitive intelligence. We discovered there was even an industry association called Strategic and Competitive Intelligence Professionals. The members of the organization have written countless articles and books defining CI, its processes, and procedures. Over the years they created a list of commonly applied techniques to legally and ethically gather information on the competition and convert it into intelligence. Howard and I recognized that many of the techniques they described were similar to those used by investigative journalists. With my background, it was a natural fit."

"I had no idea," Jack said. "So if competitive intelligence is something so widely embraced by academics, why the negative public perception? Why is it confused with corporate espionage?"

Laurence pushed his plate aside and put his elbows up on the table. "One of the most popular books on the subject of competitive intelligence was published in 1992—*CIA, Inc.: Espionage and the Craft of Business Intelligence*. It was written by a former U.S. intelligence officer. Despite the fact that the book details straightforward legal and ethical competitive intelligence techniques, the link to CIA activities and the word 'espionage' in the title muddied the waters a bit."

"You can't get more cloak-and-dagger than the CIA," Jack said.

Laurence sighed. "Then of course there have been a handful of people that have engaged in real corporate espionage under the banner of competitive intelligence. One knucklehead even published a book talking about all the dirty tricks he pulled. Shame. Anytime something like that happens, it sets the entire practice back *years*. And it makes companies with legitimate CI functions think twice about going public, for fear of a backlash."

"So that's why things were kept so quiet at Hewitt, why you were such a mystery man at the company."

"Bingo," Laurence said. "As much as I wanted to integrate CI throughout the entire organization, Howard thought it just wasn't worth the risk."

Jack pushed his plate aside, and both men were quiet for a time as they digested their meals and their thoughts. When the waiter arrived with the check, Laurence dropped some cash into the billfold and rose.

"Now, perhaps you'd like to see a few examples of competitive intelligence in action?"

Jack stood. "Ready when you are."

Laurence handed Jack the CI bible. "You're going to need this."

As they made their way to the door, Jack flipped to the second page in the little black book and read the following:

> *CI offers approximations and best views of the market and the competition. **It is not a peek at a rival's financial books**.*

CHAPTER 15

THE DOS AND DON'TS

The downtown Chicago sidewalks were packed with professionals in power ties and business suits making their way back to work after lunch. Jack Turner was bumped numerous times as he attempted to keep up with Bob Laurence while flipping through the pages of the old man's CI bible.

One section in particular had captured Jack's attention: *The Dos and Don'ts of CI*. Jack eagerly began to read, hoping the section would answer a number of questions percolating in his mind.

The Dos and Don'ts of CI

- *DO obtain information from public sources—sources that clearly have the right to provide the information.*

- *DO, when necessary, make it clear to a source that you do not want to receive confidential or proprietary information.*

- *DO test the ethics of a situation by asking, "Is it right?" before proceeding.*

- *DO collect competitor literature that is disseminated in the market.*

- *DO engage in reverse engineering of obtained products.*

- *DO be smart and cautious.*

- *DO keep good records of where the information came from, to protect against a charge of illegal or unethical conduct.*

"Sorry," Jack said as he sidestepped a woman with a large cup of coffee in each hand. He looked up and spotted Laurence nearly half a block ahead. Jack caught up with the old man at the next intersection.

"So where are we headed?" Jack asked.

"My office," Laurence replied. He pointed east. "Not far. Another two blocks down."

"Your office? What do you mean, your office?"

The light changed and the crowd of pedestrians began to hustle their way across the street.

"My super-secret underground lair, where I plot the downfall of our enemies."

Jack stopped in the middle of the street.

"Lighten up, Jack, it was a joke," Laurence said with a grin. He patted Jack on the shoulder. "Come on. I'll explain when we get there."

Jack laughed, beginning to get a feel for the old man's dry sense of humor. He followed close behind, his thoughts returning to "The Dos and Don'ts of CI." He was surprised by two of the "Dos" in particular. He flipped back to the pages and started reading them again.

- *DO keep good records of where the information came from to protect against a charge of illegal or unethical conduct.*

- *DO, when necessary, make it clear to a source you do not want to receive confidential or proprietary information.*

More than anything Laurence had said thus far, these two points began to make Jack see CI as a legitimate business function. But he also had a major question: How could you gather intelligence on the competition if you didn't accept confidential or proprietary information? Intrigued, Jack began reading the Don'ts section:

The Dos and Don'ts of CI

- *DON'T do anything that common sense says you shouldn't do.*

- *DON'T induce someone to violate an obligation of confidentiality owed to his or her employer or some other party.*

- *DON'T enter a competitor's building or other restricted area without proper authorization.*

- *DON'T assume another person's identity.*

- *DON'T use an agent or competitive intelligence firm to obtain information using means your company would not use.*

Once again, Jack felt reassured about the legitimacy of competitive intelligence. *If* Laurence followed these basic rules, what he did really was legal and ethical. On the flip side, if he did tell sources that he didn't want confidential information, if he didn't use an assumed identity, if he didn't snoop around a competitor's building, and if he didn't use others to do the snooping for him, how would he find any worthwhile information?

Jack drifted back to a sleepless night nearly two months ago, just days after Howard Hewitt's death. He remembered scouring Hewitt's database, searching for any information that would hint at a possible move by Sampson, and finding nothing. He remembered his frustration, and he clearly recalled telling his wife, "We're drowning in all this information, yet we're starving for real intelligence."

If what Laurence said was true, if he was able to achieve the types of results he claimed while following these strict rules of conduct, it would completely change the game.

Jack looked up and nearly crashed into Laurence. The old man raised an eyebrow. "Interesting read, isn't it?" he asked in his sand-and-gravel voice.

"Very," Jack replied, fanning through the pages of the little black book. "But it seems like every answer creates another question."

"The answers are all there," Laurence said. "I made sure of that. But I know what they say about proof and pudding. Come on inside, and I'll show you a few examples of CI in action. That should be proof enough."

"We're here?" Jack said, stepping back to look at the building before them. It was an old brick fire station that had evidently been converted into office space. "What, the Bat Cave was already occupied?"

Laurence smiled. "You know, Jack, I think we're going to get along just fine."

HIGHLIGHTS FROM JACK TURNER'S CI BIBLE

- *Competitive intelligence was created, in part, through Professor Michael Porter's scholarship at Harvard Business School. Porter's work was first presented over thirty years ago in the book Competitive Strategy.*

- *Since then, business leaders from across the nation, led by Strategic and Competitive Intelligence Professionals (SCIP), have built what has become known as competitive intelligence.*

- *CI is an analytical process that can transform raw data into relevant, accurate, and actionable knowledge about the market and the competition. It is not a peek at a rival's books.*

- *CI professionals DO:*

  o *Obtain information from public sources—sources that clearly have the right to provide the information*

  o *Make it clear to sources that they do not want to receive confidential or proprietary information*

  o *Test the ethics of a situation by asking, "Is it right?" before proceeding*

  o *Collect competitor literature that is disseminated in the market*

  o *Engage in reverse engineering of obtained products*

- o *Keep good records of where the information came from, to protect against a charge of illegal or unethical conduct*

- *CI professionals DO NOT:*

  - o *Do anything that common sense says they shouldn't do*

  - o *Induce sources to violate obligations of confidentiality owed to their employer or some other party*

  - o *Enter a competitor's building or restricted area without proper authorization*

  - o *Assume another person's identity*

  - o *Use agents or CI firms to obtain information through means that their own company would not use*

CHAPTER 16

IT'S A GRIND

The little boy in Jack Turner couldn't help but beam when he saw that the old fire station, despite its completely remodeled interior, still had its fire pole.

"In case of emergencies," Bob Laurence said with a smile, seeing Jack's look.

"Of course," Jack said. "You never know when the alarm will sound." He motioned around the room. "What is all this?"

"I resigned from Hewitt Games, but that doesn't mean I retired. What you see will soon become the Chicago office of a competitive intelligence firm I've worked with for a number of years now. The firm, Proactive Worldwide, heard about my resignation from Hewitt and asked if I would become the managing director of this office. I accepted."

Behind a wide front desk Jack saw rows of cubicles in the middle of a gleaming hardwood floor. Private offices lined the side and back walls.

"Great space," Jack said with a nod. "But I'm not sure I understand. You worked with a competitive intelligence firm while you were at Hewitt?"

"A good CI campaign takes hundreds of hours of hard work—more than any one person could possibly handle in any reasonable timeframe. Without the proper in-house staff, you have to outsource most of the legwork. Thankfully, there are a handful of firms out there that can carry the load. I was lucky to find one of the good ones. I worked with Proactive Worldwide on dozens and dozens of CI campaigns for Hewitt over the years."

"CI firms? Campaigns that take hundreds of hours? Color me confused," Jack said. "Don't forget, about an hour ago I thought competitive intelligence meant lying, cheating, and stealing."

Laurence clapped Jack on the back. "You're right. I've managed to get a bit ahead of myself. Let's head upstairs and go over a CI campaign in detail, to put things in perspective."

Jack followed Laurence across the room and up a spiral staircase. On the second floor, Laurence opened a door with an electronic lock and invited Jack inside. Stacks of boxes filled the room, save for a narrow path that led to a large L-shaped desk just in front of the far wall.

"Sorry for the mess," Laurence said. "The movers just dropped these off this morning, and I had them bring everything up here for security. There's a chair next to my desk. Go ahead and grab a seat."

The two men sat down on opposite sides of the desk, and Laurence booted up his computer. He adjusted his widescreen monitor so that Jack could easily see and logged in. Once online, he went to the login page for Proactive Worldwide's company intranet.

"All of our CI documentation is digital. Every campaign Hewitt ever worked on with Proactive Worldwide, it's all there." Laurence clicked through a few screens and entered half a dozen passwords before stopping at a screen filled with folders. Each folder was dated and titled.

"The system is simple," he said. "Each folder contains detailed information about a specific CI case. In each folder there's an overview document. It's basically a case study—it defines the problem, outlines the action we took using CI, and then summarizes the results. Lots of good tidbits in there. Then there are source files. Everyone we talked to about this specific issue—name, rank, serial number, the whole nine yards. Got it?"

"Simple enough," Jack said. "But before you crack one of these files open, there's one question I've been dying to ask. How is it possible to get anything useful if you're upfront about who you are and you don't accept the confidential stuff?"

"I'm glad you asked," Laurence replied as he turned to face Jack. "A wise man once said, 'Where money changes hands, so does information.' Anytime one company pays another for products or services, information is exchanged. It's at those points, where money and information change hands, that a company's secret information begins to become private information. Now, for the most part, much of the truly private stuff is still out of bounds. But eventually, as private information continues to change hands or trickle down the supply chain, it enters the public realm. Nine times out of ten, secret information will become private information. And ten times out of ten, that private information will eventually become public information. And just because information isn't published doesn't mean it isn't publicly available. You just have to ask for it."

"So you contact a company's suppliers directly?"

"Among a great many other types of sources, absolutely. We call them touch points, or sweet spots."

"And you tell them who you are?"

"It would be unethical to do otherwise," Laurence said.

"And they *still* give you information?"

Laurence laughed. "A big part of it is in the approach and the types of questions you ask, no doubt. You can't just pick up the phone, dial Sampson's biggest supplier, and expect someone to tell you what the company's R&D department is cooking up. But you'd be surprised, Jack. When you do the hard work—the primary and secondary research—and do it well, you'll find people who know things and are willing to talk. Once you get one tidbit of information from one person, you can build on it. And that's what real competitive intelligence is all about—finding these small pieces of data that are scattered across the supply chain. Over time, you can gather enough of them to see the big picture and create relevant, accurate, and actionable intelligence."

"I think I'm beginning to understand what you meant by hundreds of hours of work, and why you would need a helping hand," Jack said.

"It's a grind," Laurence said, grinning. "Not quite the James Bond stuff you imagined, is it?"

Jack laughed and put up his hands, "All right, all right, let's take a look at one of these case files of yours."

Laurence swiveled back to the keyboard and scrolled down through the files. "Thought you'd never ask."

CHAPTER 17

INSIDE A CI CAMPAIGN

B ob Laurence told a story as he went through the files in the folder entitled "Hewitt Games: Third-Party Controllers, August 2000."

"This is one of my favorite cases and one that demonstrates the type of work that goes into a good CI campaign," he said. "As you know, Hewitt launched the current version of the Primo game console in 2000 with a single controller instead of two because of costs. We knew customers wouldn't be thrilled, but we also recognized that the revenue opportunity we'd create by selling extra controllers was too good to pass up."

Jack remembered the strategy clearly. His department was heavily involved in the ultimate decision, providing data that clearly showed that having to buy an extra controller wouldn't deter the vast majority of consumers from purchasing a new Primo.

"But we also had to make sure we sold the controllers at the right price point and with the right features to make sure third-party manufacturers wouldn't steal our thunder," Laurence continued. "That's where I came in."

Jack sat silent, fascinated as the old man began describing the CI processes and techniques in detail.

Over the years, Laurence explained, he'd worked with Proactive Worldwide to compile a massive database of resources and contacts across the industry. To kick off the controller campaign, he worked with a team from the firm to contact all major retailers, specialty stores, and mass merchants. They tracked down stockers, store managers, inventory managers, and warehouse and distribution center managers to see if anyone could locate third-party controllers for the soon-to-be-released Primo and provide any details on the product.

Laurence described how they located buyers for every major store across the country and conducted hundreds of interviews. No one had yet seen or heard of third-party controllers for the new Primo.

"That was good news," Laurence said. "We knew that if the buyers hadn't seen anything yet, we'd still have time to tweak our own offering."

Laurence and Proactive Worldwide then began contacting the third-party manufacturers directly. They sought out sales representatives, contract salespeople, and even international representatives to see if there would be a worldwide push.

"Sales reps are born talkers, and they can be some of your best sources in any CI campaign," Laurence said. "I managed to track down some major account representatives who work with the national retail chains. I knew that if there was going to be a major launch, these national reps would be the first to roll them out."

Based on direction from these sales reps, Laurence found a third-party manufacturer that would, in fact, be releasing sales and promotional materials for its new Primo products in two months' time.

"And to think," Jack said, "I pictured you sitting in your office on the Forty-Second with your feet up on a desk and a cigar in your hand. You were a busy bee, Bob."

Laurence raised a bushy eyebrow. "What, you think that's it? Those hundreds of calls we made and countless conversations we had with stockers, store managers, distribution center managers, and sales reps were just the first line of intelligence collection."

"The first?" Jack asked.

Laurence nodded in reply.

"The first of how many?"

Laurence held up three fingers.

Jack shook his head. "Correction—you were a *very* busy bee. No wonder you and Howard got along so well."

Laurence continued the story, outlining the targets in the second line of intelligence collection: marketing companies, PR firms, ad agencies, market research firms, and media outlets.

"We knew from my earlier interviews that the third-party manufacturer was creating a whole new brand for its Primo product. This was a big red flag for Hewitt, but it also created a huge opening. As you know, branding requires an entire team of people working in conjunction with potential ad agency partners. Our database includes a directory of product managers, brand managers, and category managers for hundreds of products across the gaming industry. Once we identified the brand teams that would potentially work on this type of product, we began conducting interviews."

Through these interviews, Laurence and his team confirmed that the new brand of controllers would be launched, and they even identified ad agencies, PR firms, and market research firms that might be used to support the launch.

"After interviewing everyone and anyone we could track down at those firms, we had a strong idea what the potential differentiators of the new product would be, and that's critical," Laurence said. "Particularly when we found out we would be going up against a wireless controller."

Jack snapped his fingers. "That's why Hewitt demanded wireless for the new Primo!"

Laurence grinned. "And don't forget the entire line of rechargeable batteries and chargers to go along with it."

"Amazing," Jack said. "So we knew who we would be up against, and some critical details about the products they would be launching. But what about pricing? Who was in your third line of intelligence collection?"

"Everyone in the first line of intelligence collection."

"Not sure I follow," Jack said.

Laurence folded his hands on the desk. "As you said, we knew who and we knew what. When you have information like that, you're able to talk more confidently about the subject matter in your interviews. You're not just fishing for information—you're having a conversation among insiders. And we were on the inside. Once you're there, it's amazing how much people will open up to you and provide the bits and pieces you need to paint a much clearer picture."

Laurence picked up his desk phone but didn't dial. "Allow me to demonstrate. Let's say I just called back the category buyer for Gadgets stores. The conversation would go something like this. 'Hey, Richard, this is Bob Laurence at Hewitt. We spoke last month about those new wireless controllers for the Primo from Banditz. I'm great, how are you? That's great, Richard. Listen, have you gotten your hands on one of those new Banditz yet? You did, eh? I thought you might have—you're always ahead of the rest of the pack. Gadgets would be lost without you. What did you think of the Bandit? I always think the third-party stuff has a cheap feel to it. It's true—you get what you pay for. I heard the MSRP was all the way down around $14.99. Really, $19.99? What, do they think they're getting Howard Hewitt's seal of approval on the box? Listen, Richard, I've got to run. Keep in touch, and thanks for the info.'"

Laurence hung up the phone and ended his imaginary conversation. Jack applauded.

Laurence gave a slight bow. "So what did we learn through our competitive intelligence efforts? We discovered a company would be launching a new product that would compete directly with our own, we discovered they would differentiate themselves from Hewitt's product because they were wireless, and we discovered the MSRP was $19.99."

Jack jumped in. "And based on that intelligence, we avoided a potentially disastrous wired controller line, created an entire line of new rechargeable batteries and chargers we knew would be in demand, and priced our Hewitt controllers as premium without being excessive."

"Bingo," Laurence said. "And that line of controllers, chargers, and batteries is still making Hewitt a bundle today."

Jack eased back in his chair. "Great story, Bob. I hate to admit it, but I think I might have been wrong about competitive intelligence, about you, the whole deal. I just have one more important question that could really help me determine if this is something Hewitt should pursue."

Laurence sat forward in his seat.

"Can I slide down the fire pole?"

Laurence let loose a booming laugh. "Absolutely," he said. "And it's appropriate, because we could very well be in the middle of an emergency situation."

"Oh?" Jack said, laughing along with Laurence.

Laurence nodded as he worked out the last of his chuckles. "I got wind Sampson might be moving in for the knockout blow on Hewitt by upping the launch of their new next-generation console."

Jack burst out laughing. It would still be a good *two years* before the next new console war. Wouldn't it? When Jack saw that the old man wasn't joking, the smile abruptly fell from his face. "That can't be. Are you sure?"

"Not even close," Laurence said, deep lines appearing on his furrowed brow. "But I recommend we find out as much as we can, as quickly as we can. The future of Hewitt Games could very well be at stake."

CHAPTER 18

LIGHT READING

Andy Barrows rested his chin on his folded hands. Jack Turner, having completed his story about Bob Laurence and competitive intelligence, drummed his fingers on his knee, waiting.

"To tell the new CEO or not to tell the new CEO—that is the question," Barrows said to himself. He looked up at Jack and smiled. "Whether 'tis nobler in the office to suffer the slings and arrows of outrageous fortune—"Barrows stood now and embraced his inner thespian "—or to take arms against a sea of troubles, begin a competitive intelligence campaign, and by opposing, end the downfall of Hewitt Games."

Jack shook his head but couldn't help smiling. "I don't think you understand the gravity of this situation, Andy."

Barrows sat back down. "Sorry, it just came to me. Perfect, though, isn't it? Old Bill Shakespeare might as well have been writing about this very predicament."

"All right, then, Hamlet, what should I do?"

Barrows took a deep breath and exhaled slowly. "The first time Laurence mentioned competitive intelligence to you, how did you react?"

"You know I ran like hell," Jack said.

"And I think that's your answer," Barrows said with a shrug. "No matter how legit it may be, there's still a dark and ominous cloud hanging over competitive intelligence. I just don't think you could bring something like this to Susan Wright and not have her run you out of town. Especially not right now, not with everything that's gone on at Hewitt Games in the past few months. Uh-uh, no way."

Jack slumped back in his chair. "And if I don't go to Susan, then what? We can't just ignore the possibility that Sampson could very well be preparing to bury us. What if they were to launch a new console in 2010 and we didn't have the new Primo ready until 2011 at the earliest? We'd be sitting ducks."

"Correction," Barrows said. "Throw in the momentum Sampson is riding from ReelHD, and we'd be *dead* ducks. There's got to be a way." Barrows laced his fingers behind his head and leaned back in his executive's chair. After what seemed like an eternity to Jack, Barrows finally sat forward and spoke. "That wireless controller case file Laurence showed you, with all that specific info on whom he spoke to, what he said, what he learned—that's what you need. You need to go to Wright with irrefutable, legally and ethically obtained intelligence about this supposed new Sampson console."

"That could take months, Andy. We just don't have that kind of time. We need to act now."

"Fine, then what about the bumped-up launch? Build a perfect case file on that very specific bit of information alone, and you'll undoubtedly get Wright's attention."

Jack bolted upright. "You're right. She responded when I went to her with Sampson's plans for June 23. She nearly fired me on the spot when she found out that all I had was the date and no evidence to back it up. But if we can go back to her with all the proof she needs *and* with detailed records on how we obtained the information—"

"Then she couldn't possibly have you escorted out of the building by security," Barrows chimed in. "Unless of course you let your department go to hell while you're off tilting at windmills."

Jack jumped from his seat and headed for the door.

"Hey, wait, buddy, I was just kidding."

Jack turned back. "I know. This isn't me storming out—this is me realizing I've got more work than one man can handle and a ticking time bomb of a deadline."

* * *

Back in his office, Jack closed his door and sat down. Thoughts and ideas, hopes and fears raced through his mind, and one question repeated itself over and over again: *Where do I start?*

Finally, Jack took a deep breath and decided to follow the advice that Bob Laurence had given in parting. Jack opened his jacket, took the CI bible from his breast pocket, and began to read.

As he flipped through the pages, Jack began highlighting the entries that helped create a clearer definition of competitive intelligence:

> *Competitive intelligence is (1) information that has been analyzed to the point where you can make a decision; (2) an early warning tool to alert management of both threats and opportunities; and (3) a means to deliver reasonable assessment.*

> *Competitive intelligence helps to avoid surprises, helps improve short- and long-term planning, and allows companies to gain and maintain a competitive edge.*

> *Paper information, electronic data, and traditional market research are only one part of the intelligence equation. CI is people actively investigating the competition by talking to other people.*

Jack liked that line and underlined it for good measure: <u>CI is people actively investigating the competition by talking to other people.</u> He read on, continuing to highlight the snippets that rang true:

> *Competitive intelligence tracks incremental shifts in the business environment on a regular basis, keeping a company from being caught by surprise and swept away by unexpected and lethal changes. Continual, ongoing monitoring of the competition is a must.*

> *Competitive intelligence is designed to help its users ferret out hard-to-find facts and bridge the gap between guessing and knowing, so a*

company can more accurately predict events in the marketplace, not as futurists, but as realists.

Effective results are probable, not just possible, when CI is used properly.

More confident about CI's purpose and power, Jack reread all of the entries he'd highlighted and began sorting through the pearls of wisdom that would help jump-start his own CI project:

The goal of every CI project is to gain perspective, not statistical accuracy. This is a critical distinction between traditional market research and competitive intelligence. CI offers qualitative versus quantitative information. It delivers pointed and useful insights drawn from a carefully mined group of sources.

Be specific about the project's scope. Don't try to "get whatever you can." Work hard to clearly define a focused project objective and gain an understanding of how the information gathered will be used to impact a decision.

Set realistic timeframes. Good, fast, or cheap— pick two.

Good intelligence cannot be obtained just by sitting down at a computer, punching some buttons, and waiting for information to pop out. It takes time to speak to enough knowledgeable sources to piece together the puzzle and form an appropriate conclusion and action recommendation.

Ask, "Can it be done?" Estimate the percentage of intelligence that can actually be gathered before proceeding. Be sure that the research can be done legally and ethically.

Jack's confidence continued to grow with each streak of his green highlighter. His initial CI project had a clearly defined goal: find out if Sampson was bumping up the launch date of its new console, and if so, by how much.

Jack was also confident that it could be done. If Sampson was getting an early jump on a new console, Hewitt's rival would have to work with a number of producers and suppliers. The amount of intelligence that could be gathered on such a project was abundant.

Jack read on, suddenly sure that his CI project would be a rousing success. He began envisioning a celebratory toast with Hewitt's board of directors, a promotion, and a spur-of-the-moment tropical vacation with Sofia and the kids. The daydream ended when Jack turned to one of the final pages in the CI bible:

> *WARNING: When born during a "Big Bang event," a company's CI program is immediately set up for failure. By launching into mission-impossible tasks within a we-need-it-yesterday timeframe, the outcome is inevitably disappointing.*

CHAPTER 19

AND THEN THERE WERE THREE

When Bob Laurence answered the phone, Jack Turner didn't even bother saying hello.

"When born during a Big Bang event, a company's CI program is immediately set up for failure?"

"So you read the book," Laurence replied. "Good."

"Yes, I read the book. And I'd like to know why you decided to end it on such a low note. You do realize we're in the middle of the biggest Big Bang event this company has seen in the last twenty years, don't you?"

"Of course I do. And I left that bit of information for last to get your attention. I see that it did."

If Jack had been near a mirror, he was sure he would have seen smoke coming out of his ears.

"You spend all this time trying to get me on board, and when you finally do, you tell me I'm doomed?"

"You're not doomed," Laurence said, his rough voice calm. "Hewitt's CI program isn't being born out of this Big Bang. It already exists, and you'll have access to the database I spent years of my professional life creating, the proven processes and techniques, and my expertise every step of the way."

Jack shook his head. "Now you're really confusing me."

"Then let me clarify. CI isn't just some strategy-of-the-month gimmick. It's not a tool you can pick up at your discretion and use, a hammer that pounds down loose nails. We will get over this particular obstacle, Jack. But what happens at Hewitt Games when the next bull comes charging and I'm not there with my red cape? Will Hewitt see it coming or get skewered by Sampson's horns?"

Jack felt the anger draining out of his system as Laurence's meaning became clear.

"The point I'm trying to make is that this isn't a one-time thing, especially not in today's hypercompetitive business environment," Laurence continued. "If you go back to business as usual after this event, you'll only succeed in delaying failure. Your unenviable task is not only to help the company get through this particular Big Bang, but also to convince Susan Wright that a full-time competitive intelligence function is essential to Hewitt Games' success."

"That's all?" Jack said. "You should know that I already decided not to let her in on this until we have something concrete on Sampson pushing up its new console launch."

"I can understand why," Laurence said. "That means we'll have to get started immediately. And we could use an extra set of hands. I can bring Proactive Worldwide on board, but having another in-house person would be a huge help. Got any bright overachievers in your department who are good on the phone and would be open to something like this?"

"Slow down a minute, would you?" Jack said. "I just signed myself up for CI duty today, and I'm not even sure *I'm* the right man for the job. And just how do you plan on paying an outside firm to get involved? There's no way I could get a budget for this, and don't forget, you resigned from Hewitt."

"And I signed with Proactive Worldwide. As part of my agreement with the firm, Hewitt is entitled to one free, very targeted CI campaign—nothing too expensive or time-consuming. I figured if I couldn't get you on board, I would reach out to Susan Wright with a freebie, see if I could open up her eyes to CI that way."

"I guess you covered all of your bases," Jack said, stunned.

"By failing to prepare, you are preparing to fail, as Ben Franklin wrote," Laurence said. "And don't worry, Jack—you are the right man for the job. You've got the experience, the skill set, and the work ethic. I wouldn't have picked you otherwise. Now, time is of the essence. We're not in a mission-impossible scenario, but the clock is ticking. How about that extra set of hands?"

Jack took a deep breath and did his best to clear his thoughts. When he did, a name appeared instantly: Julie Sawyer.

* * *

Jack Turner remembered what Julie Sawyer had described as her strongest trait in their first interview together, and he was curious whether Julie remembered it as well.

"Never saying, 'That's not my job,'" Sawyer said, sitting in front of Jack's desk.

Jack nodded in affirmation. Sawyer appeared to be the perfect candidate for the job: she was hungry, humble, and intelligent, and she hadn't been with the company long enough to find a comfort zone that she felt wary about leaving.

Jack proceeded to tell Sawyer his entire tale, from Howard Hewitt's death all the way through to Bob Laurence and learning the truth about competitive intelligence. When he was through, nearly twenty minutes had ticked off the TAG Heuer his father had given him when Jack graduated from B-school.

"Today, this company faces one of its greatest challenges, one which I could easily shrug off and not worry about because it's not my job," Jack said. "But I care too much about this organization to do that, and I will face this challenge, even if it means stepping outside of my official role and responsibilities."

"And you'd like me to help?" Sawyer asked enthusiastically.

Jack laughed. "I would. But I would also completely understand if it was something you didn't feel comfortable doing. Just yesterday *I* was convinced that competitive intelligence was about dumpster diving and recording conversations."

"I'm in," Sawyer replied without hesitation. "I actually had an interesting class on persuasion in B-school, and the professor talked about competitive intelligence quite a bit. I'm honored that you would ask me to help."

"That's the best news I've heard in months," Jack said as he glanced at his watch. His eyes went wide when he saw it was nearly 7:30 PM. "And it's nice to end what has been one of the longest days of my life on such an upbeat note. Sorry to have kept you so long—I completely lost track of time."

"Not a problem," Julie said. "So when do we get started on this competitive intelligence project?"

"First thing tomorrow morning," Jack replied. "You and I will be the exclusive attendees at Bob Laurence's first competitive intelligence seminar."

HIGHLIGHTS FROM JACK TURNER'S CI BIBLE

Competitive intelligence is (1) information that has been analyzed to the point where you can make a decision; (2) an early warning tool to alert management of both threats and opportunities; and (3) a means to deliver reasonable assessment.

Competitive intelligence helps to avoid surprises, helps improve short- and long-term planning, and allows companies to gain and maintain a competitive edge.

Paper information, electronic data, and traditional market research are only one part of the intelligence equation. CI is people actively investigating the competition by talking with other people.

Competitive intelligence tracks incremental shifts in the business environment on a regular basis, keeping a company from being caught by surprise and swept away by unexpected and lethal changes. Continuous, ongoing monitoring of the competition is a must.

Competitive intelligence is designed to help its users ferret out hard-to-find facts and bridge the gap between guessing and knowing, so a company can more accurately predict events in the marketplace, not as futurists, but as realists.

Effective results are probable, *not just* possible, *when CI is used properly.*

The goal of every CI project is to gain perspective, not statistical accuracy. This is a critical distinction between traditional market research and competitive intelligence. Competitive intelligence offers qualitative versus quantitative information. It delivers pointed and useful insights drawn from a carefully mined group of sources. Answers to research questions often have to be deduced or figured out.

Be specific about the project's scope. Don't try to "get whatever you can." Work hard to clearly define a focused project objective.

WARNING: When born during a "Big Bang event," a company's CI program is immediately set up for failure. By launching into mission-impossible tasks within a we-need-it-yesterday time frame, the outcome is inevitably disappointing.

PART 3

FIXING THE ROOF: DON'T WAIT UNTIL IT LEAKS

CHAPTER 20

GETTING STARTED

"Class is in session," Bob Laurence said, standing in front of Jack Turner and Julie Sawyer on the open floor of the downtown fire-station-turned-office-building.

Laurence turned and began writing on the whiteboard behind him. With a black marker he spelled out and underlined two words that Jack sensed would change his professional life forever:

COMPETITIVE INTELLIGENCE

Laurence started at the beginning, providing a definition of CI and discussing its development, going in-depth on many of the points Jack had highlighted in the CI bible. Conveniently, Laurence had also created packets for Jack and Julie to follow along. They gave Jack the distinct impression that this was information Laurence had been hoping to share with others at Hewitt Games for a long, long time.

After the CI overview, Laurence ventured into a category that Jack had been hoping he would address.

"What is illegal in CI?" Laurence asked. "Two things you need to know inside and out—one is the Uniform Trade Secrets Act, which is conveniently incorporated into the federal criminal statute you will come to know and love, the Economic Espionage Act of 1996. You'll find copies of the EEA in your packet. To cut through the legal mumbo-jumbo for you, information that is clearly secret or confidential is off-limits, and you can't steal to get it, but you are allowed to figure secrets out. It's also critical to note that the trade secret law requires a company to take reasonable measures to protect information it considers secret or confidential."

"Question," Julie said, looking up from her packet. "How do we navigate what appears to be a substantial gray area?"

"Good question," Laurence replied. "That's where the CI bible comes in. In your packets I've included everything in that book I created for Jack. These are the processes, procedures, and best practices that have been developed over the past thirty years. Follow the rules outlined in the CI bible, and you'll be fine. Consider it your legal and ethical compass."

Laurence had them flip to the CI bible section in their packets and Jack's favorite, the Dos and Don'ts of CI. "The bottom line," Laurence said after going through each line, "is to use good old-fashioned common sense. Ask yourself, if the *Tribune* were to publish an article on what we did to obtain this information, would we want people to read it?"

"It's nice to have things spelled out so clearly," Julie said.

"Having a firm set of guidelines, processes, and procedures is essential to the success of any CI project," Laurence replied with a nod. "Which brings me to my next subject ..."

They next tackled what Laurence described as the steps in the CI Cycle. "The cycle starts by understanding needs of the internal stakeholders, or how the information impacts strategy," he said. "We then create a knowledge base, collect intelligence, make intelligence actionable, and disseminate it to decision-makers. After that we obtain feedback and start all over again. Here's a diagram that shows how it works."

CI Cycle

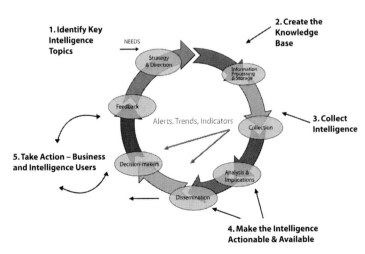

86

Jack flipped to the page in his packet and followed along. Along with bullet points describing the cycle, Laurence listed the rough percentage of time in the entire campaign that should be dedicated to each task:

1. *Plan strategy and set clear goals (10%)*

2. *Conduct secondary research: published information (15%)*

3. *Conduct primary research: external sources and CI activities (35%)*

4. *Process, analyze, and write up findings (30%)*

5. *Report findings and interact with management (10%)*

"We have a very specific goal with this project, and that's a good thing," Laurence said. "We want to find out if Sampson is upping its launch for a new console, and if so, by how much of a time frame? We already have all of the traditional market research info we could possibly need, thanks to the work of your fine department, Jack. What we've really got to focus on, and get you up to speed on as quickly as possible, is primary research—using CI techniques to actively mine external sources. A good place to start is to talk about possible contacts that are important to strong primary research."

Jack flipped ahead in the packet to the list of potential external sources:

Advertising firms
Advertising and promotional design agencies
Allied and partner firms
Architectural firms
Associations
Auditors
Bankers
Benefits companies
Brokerage industry analysts
Building managers
Business park managers
Commercial property agents
Complementary product manufacturers
Construction management firms
Consumer advocates
Contract sales force members
Contractors
Customers
Direct competitors
Distributors
Domain name registration agencies
Educational institutions
End-user organizations and forums
End users

Equipment dealers, installers, and manufacturers
Ex-employees
Foreign branch offices
Human resource agencies
Internet service providers
Inventors of similar products
Initial public offering underwriters
Journalists
Key opinion and thought leaders
Labor union officials
Lawyers
Local sources: chambers of commerce, dining and entertainment venues, document prep shops, lodging establishments, and vocational programs
Market research companies
Media buying firms
Neighboring entities and persons
OEMs
Outside consultants
Outsourced call centers
Package designers
Packagers
PR agencies

Published and syndicated report authors
Raw materials suppliers
Recent interns
Regulatory agencies
Relatives
Repair and warranty facilitators
Research institutions
Retailers
Returned product handlers
Subcomponent and subassembly companies
Subsidiaries
Suppliers
Telecom providers
Temp staffing agencies
Topic-specific chat rooms
Trade experts
Trade organizations
Trademark and patent registration agencies
Transportation companies
Value-added resellers
Warehousing agents
Waste management firms
Web site designers
Wholesalers

"We've got our work cut out for us," Jack said, thinking of the hundreds of companies that could be involved.

"My neck hurts just from reading this list," Julie said with a laugh. "I can imagine what it will feel like after craning to hold a phone for dozens of hours on end."

"Now, now, my wary CI students," Laurence said. "Because our project is so focused, we already know we won't have to contact three-quarters of the types of companies on this list. And we will have the help of my CI firm along the way. What you should be worrying about is how you'll speak with the companies you do contact to elicit the kind of information we're looking for."

Jack folded his arms across his chest. "Sounds to me like you're about to share the real CI goods with us."

Laurence grinned. "Indeed."

HIGHLIGHTS FROM JACK TURNER'S CI BIBLE

Uniform Trade Secrets Act

> *It is illegal to acquire, disclose, or use a trade secret that was acquired by improper means.*

> *Improper means include theft, bribery, misrepresentation, breach, or inducement of a breach of a duty to maintain a secret.*

Economic Espionage Act of 1996 (federal criminal statute)

> *It is a federal criminal act to steal a trade secret to one's own benefit or the benefit of others.*

CHAPTER 21

ELICITATION TECHNIQUES

"Before we move on, let me ask you a question, Jack," Bob Laurence said, capping his marker and taking a seat at the table with Jack Turner and Julie Sawyer. "Have I ever told you how much I hated working at Hewitt Games?"

Jack and Julie turned to look at one another in disbelief. Jack looked back at Laurence. "Come again?"

Laurence didn't blink. "Did you know I hated working at Hewitt?"

"N-no," Jack finally managed. "I had no idea. In fact, I thought you loved working at Hewitt. What exactly did you hate about it?"

"Howard being an unreasonable tyrant, for starters. I loved the man like a brother, but God help me if he wasn't the worst SOB in this city to work with."

"They didn't call him the Bobby Knight of business for nothing," Jack said with an unsure smile. "But if you hated it so much, why did you stay on for so many years?"

"Don't get me wrong—I loved what I did, and I loved working in this industry. But working with Howard could be downright torturous. You're lucky—you've got an employees' CEO now in Susan Wright. I just read an article that said she was making Hewitt Games a kinder, gentler place to work."

"It's not all sugar and spice, believe me," Jack said, shaking his head. "Susan Wright is an open communicator, and she trusts department heads to make their own decisions, but she's not soft. She made it crystal clear to me that she *will* hold people accountable for their decisions."

"Clear to *you*?" Laurence's face showed pure disbelief. "You're a star at that company, Jack. Everyone knows you lead the best market research department in the business."

"That's very kind of you," Jack said. "But you know better than anyone how good CI made my department look."

"Nonsense," Laurence said, waving a dismissive hand. "As you saw in my CI Cycle diagram, traditional market research plays a critical role in intelligence gathering. Thanks to your department's work, my job was much easier, believe me. But enough about that. I'm curious what exactly Susan Wright made clear to you."

"She questioned my judgment in going to her with the June 23 warning without anything tangible to back it up. She didn't mince words when she said that if I pulled something like that again, I'd be looking for a new job the next day."

Laurence smiled. "So the new boss isn't as different from the old boss as I thought. I can imagine you saw her temper flare again when Sampson announced ReelHD."

"She was fired up, no doubt. But it was all about working the problem, not trying to lay blame."

"Working the problem. So I guess that means we'll be seeing an HD movie player from Hewitt in the not-too-distant future."

"Possibly," Jack said. "I wouldn't bet on it, though. We're working on it, but I think Sampson is just too far ahead of us on this one."

"Surely Hewitt could get their own HD player to market in six months, a year tops?"

"Closer to a year," Jack said. "Like I said, Sampson was way out in front on this one. They'll have that market to themselves for a good long time—an eternity in this business."

Laurence stood. "Good. Let's stop right there and talk about the elicitation techniques I used to find out that Sampson will have the HD movie market to themselves for a good year."

Julie laughed. "I was wondering what that little heart-to-heart was all about."

"A demonstration," Laurence said with a wink.

"I knew something was rotten in Denmark," Jack said. "You didn't really hate working at Hewitt, did you?"

"There was truth in what I said, but you've correctly pointed out the first elicitation technique I used."

Laurence turned and wrote on the whiteboard:

1. Provocative Statement

"A provocative statement is highly disarming, and it's a tool that's used to set the stage for an entire conversation," Laurence continued. "It deflects attention away from the core issue you want to address. The intent is to get the person you're speaking with to ask you a question, as Jack did nicely when he asked what I hated about working at Hewitt."

"Clever," Julie said. "Getting the person to ask you questions makes them think they're leading the conversation."

"Precisely," Laurence said. "And the entire time, it is actually *you* who is gently pushing the conversation toward the topic you want to address."

Laurence turned back to the board and wrote:

2. Quid pro Quo

"The second technique is the old 'I'll show you mine if you show me yours.' When used with a strong provocative statement, you can really get the people you're speaking with to open up and start talking about themselves. I opened up to Jack, telling him why I hated working at Hewitt Games. Now, before Jack reciprocated, I made sure to give him a little direction with our third technique."

3. Quotation of Reported Facts

"When you said you read somewhere that Susan Wright was making Hewitt a kinder, gentler place to work," Jack said.

"Correct," Laurence said. "Say you read something somewhere or saw a report on television, and the person you're speaking with understands it to be in the public domain. I used this tool to transition the conversation to Hewitt's current leadership, and Jack nicely played the quid pro quo part and shared information about Susan Wright."

"Always happy to play the human guinea pig," Jack said.

Laurence grinned. "You couldn't have played it any better. Let's look at the next four techniques I used to elicit information."

4.   *Word Repetition*

5.   *Flattery*

6.   *Feigned Disbelief*

7.   *Feigned Naiveté*

"When Jack said Susan Wright made it 'clear to him,' I saw the perfect opening for word repetition," Laurence continued. "It's a simple technique that tells the person you're listening and encourages them to provide more detail. And by combining that with some flattery and feigned disbelief—praising the work of Jack's department and feigning disbelief that Susan Wright would ever criticize it—I simultaneously got Jack to open up a bit more while nudging him closer to the real topic I wanted to address."

"ReelHD," Julie said.

"More precisely, I wanted to know if and when Hewitt would launch an HD player of its own," Laurence said. "I repeated some of the above techniques before I had the perfect opening to go for the jugular." Laurence turned and wrote on the whiteboard:

8.   *Bracketing Techniques*

"When you said Hewitt should be able to get an HD player to market in six months to a year," Jack said.

"You're both picking this up quickly," Laurence said with a nod. "Provide the person with a wide but realistic range of numbers, and more times than not, they'll fill in the blanks, as Jack did when he said it would be a year at least."

"Giving you precisely the information you were looking for, without Jack even realizing it," Julie said.

"No fair," Jack said with a smile. "He was using Jedi mind tricks."

"And soon you will be too. This is what professional CI firms do every day," Laurence said, reaching down into a box beside the table. He removed two copies of a book and laid them in front of Jack and Julie. "John Nolan is a former intelligence officer turned consultant and author. His book, *Confidential*, details all of the elicitation techniques I went over today, and much more. Read as much of it as you can tonight, and we'll work on your elicitation skills tomorrow."

"When do you think we'll be ready to start on the project?" Julie asked.

"I'm shooting for next week," Laurence replied. "The plan is to get you two primed and ready to mine the intel at one of the richest resources in the industry: the Electronic Gaming Expo."

"A week," Julie said, her shoulders slumping. "I wish we had longer."

"At least we won't have to go far," Jack offered. "This year's expo is right here in the Windy City."

HIGHLIGHTS FROM JACK TURNER'S CI BIBLE

Effective Elicitation Techniques

1. *Provocative Statement: highly disarming, it can get people talking and shift the perception of who is leading the conversation*

2. *Quid pro Quo: something for something. Share information to gain information.*

3. *Quotation of Reported Facts: places the subject matter in the public domain*

4. *Word Repetition: shows you are listening and can guide the conversation in a specific direction*

5. *Flattery: will get you everywhere. Best when a female is speaking with a male source.*

6. *Feigned Disbelief: can place you firmly on the same side as your source*

7. *Feigned Naiveté: means that if someone feels like they can talk down to you, don't fight it; use it to your or your client's advantage*

8. *Bracketing Techniques: provide a wide but realistic range of data to find specific details*

CHAPTER 22

A LEAD

Jack Turner took a deep breath as he walked down the crowded grand concourse of the McCormick Place convention center. Finally, it was time.

For a full week, Jack had eaten, drank, and slept competitive intelligence. And he'd practiced elicitation techniques with Bob Laurence and Julie Sawyer until the conversations had become mental chess matches—a series of well-thought-out moves with a single goal: checkmate.

With the tools of competitive intelligence at his disposal, Jack felt anxious to take his knowledge from the classroom to the real world. His excitement turned to wonder as he walked into the 840,000-square-foot convention center.

"This never gets old," Jack said to himself.

Color, light, and sound danced all across the stadium-like hall in a dizzying spectacle of technology. Console developers, game studios, suppliers, marketing and PR firms, licensing agents—anyone and everyone in the video game industry was here, set up in elaborate booths as far as the eye could see.

Jack made his way through the crowd to the Hewitt booth, which featured a massive video wall playing clips from Primo's most popular titles. He found Bob Laurence and Julie Sawyer chatting nearby.

"What held you up?" Laurence asked, glancing at his watch.

"My other job," Jack said. "Susan Wright wants complete reports on ReelHD by next week, and I had to jumpstart our market research efforts to properly gauge consumer response."

"What are people saying so far?" Laurence asked.

"Anecdotally, the initial response is positive," Jack said. "It's easy to use, and the image quality is impressive. We'll have some hard data from our testing sites in the next few days."

"Not much we can do about ReelHD, so let's get focused on what we can accomplish today. A few things to keep in mind," Laurence held out a hand and began counting off items on his fingers. "One—this is our first line of investigation, so we're looking for leads. Remember, real CI is not about stumbling upon the Golden Fleece in a single conversation. Two—leave your ego at the door. You're not too big or important to speak with anyone, and if someone feels like they can talk down to you, don't fight it—exploit it. Remember, naiveté can be a powerful elicitation technique. Three—be flexible. Different conversations and personalities will require different techniques. Use all the different tools in your toolbox to properly elicit information."

Jack and Julie nodded in reply. Both were already thinking about the companies and people they would be chatting with today. Laurence had issued assignments to keep everyone from crossing paths and duplicating efforts. Julie would focus on game developers, Jack on suppliers, and Laurence on the competition itself: Sampson.

"Any last-minute questions?" Laurence asked. "Good. We'll rendezvous for lunch at one o'clock and swap notes. Good luck."

* * *

Jack approached the section of booths that the industry suppliers had staked out, hoping that an employee of one of the leading chip, graphics card, or peripherals manufacturers would provide a few leads. Instead, he found himself overwhelmed by sales representatives hoping to get a foot in the door at Hewitt.

Having learned his lesson, Jack switched gears when he approached a representative from the graphics card manufacturer Zero G. "I forgot how aggressive some of these vendors can be," Jack said, smiling as he shook hands with a man whose nametag read Mark Millings. "I think I just signed up for a lifetime subscription to *Gaming Monthly,* and I already receive a dozen copies in my office every month. Some people just won't take no for an answer."

"I promise not to try to sell you anything," Mark, a young man with a square jaw and an athletic build, replied. He quickly looked down at Jack's nametag. "Unless, of course, Hewitt is buying?"

"Sorry, can't help you there," Jack said, mentally sorting through his CI toolbox. It was time for a little quid pro quo. "I run the market research department, so I'm about as far away from buying and contracts as you can get. Besides, I don't think we'll be in the market for a new graphics card for a long time. Howard passing, new CEO, Sampson launching ReelHD … we've got our hands full."

"Seems like it's been a tough quarter for Hewitt," Mark said with a nod. "So what brings you over to the Zero G booth?"

"Always nice to meet people in the industry," Jack replied. "Particularly when they're on the cutting edge with a company like Zero G. Didn't I read somewhere you guys have a big new card coming out soon?"

"We do," Mark said, his eyes lighting up. "There's a fan built right into it, really keeps the temp down. And it needs it. The card is a monster—eats up pixels and spits them out." Mark's brow furrowed. "I didn't realize we'd announced that yet, especially with the union and management at each other's throats again—surprise, surprise."

Jack resisted the urge to hammer Mark with questions and opted for another elicitation technique. "At each other's throats?"

"Same old story from the union. 'What have you done for us lately?' Although I guess it's tough to blame the union too much on this one, with all the extra hours the plant had to put in to meet Sampson's crazy deadline for ReelHD."

Jack's mind began to race. The R&D department at Hewitt was still putting together its report on a reverse-engineered ReelHD system. Jack hadn't known that Zero G was one of Sampson's major suppliers on the project.

"I know what that's like," Jack began, setting up a bracketing technique. "Howard Hewitt was famous for changing deadlines at the drop of a hat. If there's one way to rile up front-line employees, it's to give them a deadline and then cut it in half without warning. Sampson's original deadline went from what, a year to six months?"

"It's … complicated," Mark said, pursing his lips. "I'd say more, but you being from Hewitt and all, I'm sure you understand."

"Oh, absolutely," Jack said, a bit deflated.

The Zero G rep stepped away to greet another attendee. Despite the abrupt ending to the conversation, Jack left with a huge boost of confidence. He'd just used the elicitation techniques he'd practiced for countless hours to find real data. Just what this info on Sampson, ReelHD, and Zero G might mean in the grand scheme of things, he had no idea. But Jack did know one thing for sure: he had a solid lead.

CHAPTER 23

DOUBLE DUTY

After nearly a full day at the Gaming Expo, Jack Turner, Julie Sawyer, and Bob Laurence returned to the future Chicago office of Proactive Worldwide. All three were tired but enlivened, and they diligently documented their work.

Going through the dozens of conversations they'd each had, a handful of leads emerged. The two most promising leads came from Jack and Julie. Laurence had been stonewalled by everyone he spoke with from Sampson—a strong sign, he said, that the company had something in the works.

Along with Jack's lead on Zero G, which Laurence assessed as "very promising," Julie had learned that one of the industry's biggest game developers, Storm Studios, appeared to have something big in the pipeline. If it had been with Hewitt, Jack and Julie already would have heard about it.

"This is a huge red flag," Laurence said, jotting notes on the whiteboard. "Every great new console needs an exclusive title at launch. If Sampson is already trying to get Storm on board, it could mean they're much farther ahead in this process than we initially believed."

"You're right," Jack said, his jaw dropping. "Storm can't design an exclusive title for Sampson's new system—"

"Unless they know the system they're designing it for," Julie jumped in.

"Correct," Laurence said. "We're making a huge leap here, based on the actual intelligence. But this is obviously a lead we have to nail down as quickly as possible."

"What's the next step?" Jack asked.

"We do some additional research and have our CI firm get on the phones," Laurence replied. "So make sure you both get your beauty sleep tonight. Tomorrow is going to be a long day."

* * *

As much as Jack would have loved to drive home and spend the evening with Sofia and the kids, he still had work to do. He walked into the office just as most Hewitt employees were leaving for the night.

After tracking his department's progress on the ReelHD project, replying to e-mail, and returning phone calls, Jack slumped back in his chair, exhausted. It was nearly 9:00 PM, and he'd been at it since 6:00 AM. A moment later, his phone rang.

"I thought I might catch you back in the office," Andy Barrows said. "How did it go at the show today, marathon man?"

"It was a long day but a good one," Jack replied. He detailed some of the conversations he'd had and the major leads they'd unearthed.

"Wow," Andy said. "You're really doing this CI thing, aren't you?"

"I am," Jack said with a yawn. "And I've got to tell you, it's some pretty powerful stuff. It's not about sitting back, ordering reports, surfing the Internet, and making your best guess. It's about getting out there and actively working to find the facts."

"We're going to have to start calling you Joe Friday," Barrows laughed. "Just the facts, ma'am."

"Very funny," Jack said. "But I guess it does feel a bit like detective work. Speaking of detective work, I'd better get going before Sofia hires someone to try and track me down."

After saying good-bye to Barrows, Jack called his wife and let her know he was on his way home. The conversation was short, and Jack could tell Sofia wasn't happy about his recent string of fifteen-hour days.

"Believe me, I would much rather be home with you and the kids all these extra hours," Jack said. "It won't be for much longer, honey, I promise."

"That's what I'm counting on," Sofia said with a sigh. "See you soon. Love you."

"Love you too," Jack said and hung up. He sighed and rubbed at the cramp that had taken up residence. He finally grabbed his jacket and headed for the door, knowing he would have to do it all over again tomorrow.

CHAPTER 24

WORKING THE PHONES

Bob Laurence had desks, Internet-ready computers, and phone lines ready and waiting for Jack and Julie the next morning. Jack was most excited about the fresh pot of coffee.

Laurence detailed the work ahead and gave Jack and Julie a primer on using the database he'd built over the years with Proactive Worldwide. After a brief training session on the database, it was time to start making calls.

It was a frustrating morning for Jack. He called all around the Zero G corporate office in New York, trying to find someone to speak with. The one executive who did take his call was friendly but firm: Zero G had nothing to say about its relationship with Sampson.

In the afternoon, Jack took a different approach, making calls directly to Zero G's plant in California, hoping to find a manager willing to talk. He ended up being shuffled around by receptionists and secretaries and making little headway.

"You're moving in the wrong direction," Laurence said when Jack finally asked for some advice. "You don't have enough information to speak with executives and managers. Start at the bottom—front-line employees—and as you gather intel, work your way up the corporate ladder. Remember, once you actually know something, you'll be on the inside. And when you're on the inside, people will open up to you."

"How am I supposed to track down a front-line employee to speak with?" Jack asked.

"Does Zero G have an employee newsletter?" Laurence replied.

"Not sure …" Jack said, sliding back behind his desk. A quick search of Zero G's Web site, and Jack found what he was looking for. He downloaded a PDF of the most recent newsletter and discovered a story of a production line employee, Michael Barton, who had just celebrated ten years with Zero G.

"You're good," Jack said to Laurence. Laurence, the phone to his ear, gave a thumbs-up in reply.

Jack called Zero G's plant again and asked to speak with Michael Barton. The receptionist put him on hold before coming back on the line to let Jack know that Michael Barton was on vacation.

"Damn," Jack said, after hanging up.

"What happened?" Julie asked.

"Guy I tracked down at the plant just happens to be on vacation," Jack replied.

"Try him at home," Laurence said, the phone still at his ear. "Not you," he said into the receiver before putting his hand over it. "Look up his home number, and give him a call. He might actually be more willing to talk outside of work."

"I'll give it a shot," Jack said with a shrug. From the newsletter article, he knew that Barton was a native of the same town as Zero G's plant. After a quick call to 411, the line was ringing at the Barton residence.

"Hello?" answered a woman with a smoker's voice.

"Sorry to bother you. My name is Jack Turner. I work for Hewitt Games, and I was calling to speak with Michael Barton. Is he in?"

"Hewitt Games? What are you selling, Space Invaders?"

"No, this isn't a sales call," Jack said with a laugh. "I'm working on a research project, and I'm interested in speaking with Mr. Barton about his work at Zero G."

"Oh," the woman replied. "Well, my husband isn't home. He's actually standing in a river somewhere in Colorado with a fishing pole in his hands. His idea of a vacation."

Jack's shoulders slumped. "I was hoping to catch him. Sorry to bother—"

"It's too bad you missed him," Mrs. Barton said, cutting Jack off. "If you're doing research on Zero G, I know Michael would have been more than happy to give you an earful right now. That company just does not value its employees. Michael's been there ten years, and they're still giving him the runaround."

Jack sat forward in his seat. "I'd heard the union and management were at each other's throats over the Sampson deal."

"You heard right," Mrs. Barton said. "First it was the greatest thing that ever happened at Zero G. Management made all these promises, said if they could get the cards for that Sampson movie player done by October, there would be bonuses all around."

"By October. So originally Zero G had, what? A year to get the ReelHD cards done?"

"Not sure. Sampson gave them the contract in … January, I believe it was. Yeah, it was January, and they wanted the cards by October—not quite a year. But then Sampson gets all in a tizzy after your celebrity CEO died and cuts the deadline from October to June."

"Your husband couldn't have been happy about that," Jack said.

"He said it wasn't a matter of making the cards—it was a matter of properly testing them, taking all the bad eggs out of the bunch. By cutting the deadline in half, he said there would end up being ten to fifteen bad cards out of every thousand, instead of only one to five."

"So the employees and the union were upset because Zero G wasn't putting out quality products?"

"That was only part of it. The real problem was with the bonuses. Management didn't want to give the bonuses they promised, even though Michael and the guys were expected to do the job in half the time. And they did!"

"Doesn't make any sense," Jack said.

"That's why the union is all up in arms."

"Did Michael say why Zero G changed course on the bonuses?"

"He didn't know. He said the union leaders do, but they're still in talks with management. They don't want to say anything that would throw off the negotiations. I've got a pot that's boiling. Do you want to leave Michael a message?"

"That's okay," Jack said. "Just let him know I called, and I'll try back next week. One more thing—do you know anyone at the union?"

"I believe Ron Groves is the union rep I hear Michael talking with."

"Thanks for taking the time to speak with me today, Mrs. Barton." Jack hung up and finally noticed that Julie and Laurence were standing in front of his desk.

"Sounded like you found another nice nugget of information," Laurence said.

"I think so," Jack replied. "Something happened with Zero G and Sampson that has Zero G's union in a tizzy. It's another piece of the puzzle, to be sure. I'm just not sure how it fits."

"Keep working on Zero G," Laurence said. "You've got something to build on now. Try to use it in your conversations. See if you can get people to open up a bit more." The old man turned to Julie. "Anything yet with the game studio?"

Julie shook her head. "Lots of voicemail messages and dead ends."

"Keep at it," Laurence said, and he turned to walk back to his desk with a hop in his step. "I'm going to get Proactive Worldwide to track down Zero G's union reps."

CHAPTER 25

ACTIONABLE INTELLIGENCE

It took another two weeks and hundreds of calls and interviews to track down the bits of data they needed. As many people as there were who either didn't know anything, or knew something but weren't comfortable sharing it, there were just as many who were willing to talk. Jack Turner, Julie Sawyer, and Bob Laurence spent another week fitting all the pieces together in their report.

While the union reps at Zero G were mostly reluctant to talk, by dropping that he had spoken with Michael Barton's wife, Jack established rapport with Ron Groves at the union. And Groves did provide one very critical piece of information: the bonuses that management had promised the plant workers were tied to another big project—a project that was no longer being done by Zero G.

Jack, Julie, and Laurence immediately made the connection to Sampson. If Zero G could get the cards out for ReelHD on the shortened deadline, they surmised, Zero G would win the contract for Sampson's new console, and management would then reward its employees with a bonus. It seemed like a logical conclusion, but they still had to fill in the gaps and answer a very important question: What happened?

According to a number of sources, the cards for ReelHD went out on time, even with Sampson's dramatically reduced deadline. So why would Sampson then pull its new console contract?

"Maybe they're just not ready," Julie had offered. "Maybe Sampson decided to hold off on the new console after all."

"Our job," Laurence had replied in his rough voice, "is to take out the maybes."

And they did. With Proactive Worldwide's help, another huge piece of information was unearthed: members of the media who covered the industry revealed that Sampson wasn't happy with the cards Zero G had produced for ReelHD. Hewitt's own R&D team soon discovered what Sampson was so upset about. A significant percentage of ReelHD boxes were prone to overheating and shutting down, mainly because of flaws in ReelHD's cards.

"It's like the wife of that Zero G plant worker told me," Jack had said when they received the news. "It wasn't a matter of manufacturing the cards. The problem was in testing them. They just didn't have the time to do it properly, and now Sampson's got a malfunctioning product on its hands."

It was a small victory for Hewitt, but the critical question remained: Did rushing on ReelHD make Sampson think twice about rushing on a new console?

With Zero G out of the picture, the team focused on other graphics card manufacturers. Sampson's new console would need one, and there were only a handful of companies left that could manufacture them.

With all of the information the team had already gathered, new doors were opened. They had become "insiders," as Laurence described, and were able to pick up the trail much more easily. And the trail eventually led to SpringBoard, a card manufacturer that was suddenly turning away new business. An all-out CI press on SpringBoard and its suppliers soon revealed that the company had its hands full with a big new contract with "a major video game console developer."

Based on Hewitt's own experience developing consoles as well as further intel from primary and secondary research, Jack, Julie, and Laurence were able to determine conclusively that Sampson was hard at work on its next-generation console. And by putting together all of the pieces, they determined that Sampson would be able to launch the device a full year before Hewitt's own next-gen console.

Going over the completed report in his office, Jack's chest swelled with pride. The information contained in the file would be priceless to Hewitt's executive team and could very well save the organization an untold sum.

Jack's hand shook as he dialed Susan Wright's office. Wright was in a meeting, so Jack left an urgent message: Hewitt had another June 23 scenario on its hands. Minutes later, Jack was told to get up to the forty-second floor immediately.

"Good luck," Julie said as Jack left his office.

"Thank you," Jack said. He held up the copies of the CI report in his hand. "Thank you for everything."

After what felt like a lifetime in the elevator, the doors chimed open on the Forty-Second, and Jack was ushered into Wright's office without a wait. He found Hewitt's new CEO behind her desk, tapping away at her keyboard, the Chicago skyline at her back. She glanced at Jack as he walked in, but she didn't bother to stand and greet him.

Jack stood, the sweat starting to stand out on his brow, until Wright finally pushed her keyboard aside and motioned for Jack to take a seat.

"Before you tell me about this new June 23 scenario," Wright began, "I want you to remember what I said to you about accountability the last time this happened. You do remember, don't you, Jack?"

"The memory is etched permanently in my mind."

"Good. In that case, what have you got?"

Jack took a deep breath. "Our current long-term plans have us set to launch an all-new Primo unit in time for next holiday season. I'm here today to tell you that if we follow that course, Sampson's new system will beat us to market by a little over a year."

Wright's complexion grew three shades paler.

"I don't need to tell you that a full year's head start on our console would be disastrous for Hewitt Games," Jack continued. "Particularly after the hit we took from ReelHD."

Wright cleared her throat. "And you have *evidence* that supports this claim?"

Jack handed Wright the bound fifteen-page report. "This is a report written by myself, my colleague from market research, Julie Sawyer, and Hewitt's former senior vice president, Bob Laurence—who, as it turns out, now works for the competitive intelligence firm this company once used."

Wright dropped the report on her desk but didn't open it. "Competitive intelligence? Laurence? Jack, I'll be honest—I made a huge mistake when I never pressed you about your first revelation about Sampson. I won't make that mistake again. Yes or no—are you involved in corporate espionage?"

"No!" Jack said, holding up his hands. "Absolutely not."

"Is there anything in this report that is secret or confidential? Anything that could in any way put this company or me in any type of legal hot water whatsoever?"

"All of the information in that report was obtained legally and ethically, I swear to you," Jack said, his heart pounding in his chest. "And the report includes incredibly detailed information on the methodology we used to pull it all together while following all applicable laws and standards."

Wright tapped her French-manicured nails on her desk; Jack heard the drum line of an execution. Finally, she opened the report and began to read. Jack sat in silence, wringing his hands as Wright's expression quickly transformed from pensive to absorbed to alarmed.

"They really are going to launch this year," Wright said under her breath. She picked up her phone. "I need the executive team in the conference room right now. Tell everyone to drop what they're doing, no matter what it is. This is an emergency." She removed the phone from her ear and held up the report. "How many copies of this do you have, Jack?"

"I have a few extras in my office. I can grab—"

"And warm up the copier," Wright said into the phone. "I've got a fifteen-page report here, and I need copies for everyone."

She hung up. "Jack, you've done some amazing work here." She flipped the report open to a random page. "Like … the wife of a Zero G production floor employee … it's brilliant! How did you ever track this woman down?"

Jack couldn't help but grin as his temperature began to fall to normal levels. "It's amazing what people will share with you if you just ask."

Wright laughed out loud.

Jack smiled. "Honestly, it took a ton of work, but it never would have been possible without Bob Laurence, Julie Sawyer, and the CI firm Laurence works with. It's a long, long story, but he's been doing this kind of competitive intelligence work for Hewitt for nearly twenty-five years."

"Laurence," Wright said, a quizzical look on her face. "How is it I never heard of him?"

Jack laughed. "Like I said, it's a long story. But it all comes down to this—this company has relied on competitive intelligence to stay out in front of our competitors for two decades. There's an entire database of CI projects that proves it."

"All the proof I need is in my hand," Wright said, holding up the report.

"I'm glad you think so," Jack said. "Because the fact is, Bob Laurence may have helped us this time, but he officially resigned from Hewitt Games, and he's not coming back. Trust me—I asked. Without him, this company doesn't have a CI function."

"I don't understand," Wright said. "It wasn't part of market research?"

Jack shook his head. "A month ago I thought competitive intelligence was the cloak-and-dagger corporate espionage stuff you were worried about before you read that report. My department had nothing to do with the CI work Laurence was doing. And in order to pull off that report, Julie Sawyer and I needed Laurence's help every step of the way. Not to mention that I had to log enough extra hours to put my marriage in jeopardy."

Wright laughed. "Jack, you're hitting me with quite a bit of information here all at once."

"I know," Jack said, shaking his head. "I'm sorry. It's been a really, really long few months for me. You have no idea. All you need to know is this—this company needs a full-time CI function, and right now, we don't have it. The return on investment from this single CI project alone is off the charts, it's—"

Wright put up her hands and laughed. "Okay, Jack, okay. But let's tackle one thing at a time, shall we? Come on, I want you in on this meeting with the executive team. They'll have plenty of questions, I'm sure. It's time we found out what Hewitt Games is really made of."

CHAPTER 26

TIME FLIES

Jack Turner checked in with Proactive Worldwide's receptionist and made his way into the office, takeout bags in hand. As he shook off the snow, he paused for a moment to marvel at the buzz of activity all around him. *Time flies*, he thought.

Jack waved hello to a few of the people he'd met over the past few months and walked up the stairs to the second floor. He knocked on the door with the placard that read BOB LAURENCE, MANAGING DIRECTOR.

"Come on in," Laurence said in his sand-and-gravel voice.

"Brought lunch," Jack said, holding up the bags.

"A man after my own heart," Laurence said. "Let's eat."

Over takeout, Jack and Laurence talked about family and friends, and Laurence told a few of his classic Howard Hewitt stories before the conversation shifted to the latest developments on Hewitt's new Primo.

"We will lead the way into the digital age," Jack said. "Sampson came out with ReelHD, which, as you know, plays disks of a particular format when hooked up to their particular console. Our yet-to-be-named stand-alone device will enable consumers to download high-def and standard-definition movies via the Internet, with or without a Primo console. And we're getting ready to announce a partnership with NetFilms, meaning our users will have access to an online library of more than ten thousand movies on launch day, to rent or to buy."

"Smart," Laurence said, taking a bite of a sandwich.

"Very," Jack agreed. "The best part is, our existing Primo owners that buy this digital device will also be able to connect it to their console and download games through a service we're developing with NetFilms. Ingenious little device they're creating."

"Ingenious little profit stream, too," Laurence said. "Those movie and game rentals will add up very quickly."

"Yes, they will."

"And it will launch with the new console?"

Jack nodded. "So far, so good. We're on schedule to make it just in time for the upcoming holiday season. Susan Wright really has Hewitt running on all cylinders. She said she would tear down the silos, and she did. She's got everyone buying into the team concept and working together toward a single goal. Sampson will most likely beat us to market with their new console by a month or two, but by that time we'll have our marketing campaign in full swing. And when people see what we've got coming, I don't think they'll mind waiting a few more weeks."

"Howard would be proud," Laurence said. "How about a full-time CI function? Getting anywhere with that?"

Jack's shoulders slumped. "Wright is … receptive, but she just doesn't have the time to address it right now, with everything that's in the pipeline. But hey, I got her to hire you and Proactive Worldwide, didn't I?"

"First official client," Laurence said with a smile that quickly fell from his face. "Just don't let this slip, Jack. We can work on specific projects for Hewitt, but to really get the full benefit of competitive intelligence, you need an in-house team that integrates CI throughout the entire organization."

"You're preaching to the choir," Jack said. "I promise you I won't let this slip. We just need to get over the hump with this new console, and then I'll make sure it gets done."

"Good," Laurence said. "Because Hewitt Games may be on the right track, but if the company stands still, even for an instant, it will get run over. Strategic adaptation, Jack. That's competitive intelligence in a nutshell."

* * *

At home that night, Jack helped Sofia put the kids to bed before opening a bottle of wine.

"I like this Jack Turner," Sofia said, sipping her glass of pinot noir in front of the fireplace. "Not constantly worried about what's around the corner waiting to pounce on his beloved Hewitt Games."

"Was I really that bad?" Jack asked with a laugh.

"I may be exaggerating, but only by a whisker. If you'd known Bob Laurence was working his magic so many years ago, you wouldn't have so many gray hairs."

"You're probably right," Jack said. "It's nice to know he's still looking out for the company, even if it is on a contractual basis. I just wish the rest of the company knew about this, the proactive worldwide work we did to help keep Hewitt out in front. Beyond the executive team, Wright has really kept the company's CI work under wraps. I'm starting to think she feels the same way Howard Hewitt did about competitive intelligence."

"Worse things could happen," Sofia offered.

Jack nodded. "True. I just wish the rest of the company knew what Bob Laurence and his team did for us for all those years."

CHAPTER 27

ROI

Just over one year later, Jack Turner sat in Andy Barrows' office, each man with a copy of the latest issue of *Time* magazine in his hands. The headline on the cover said it all:

CONSOLE CRUSH

How Hewitt Games Created This Season's Hottest Hit

"That should move a few more units," Jack said, finishing up the feature first.

"Couldn't have come off any better if we had our marketing team write it themselves," Barrows said with a laugh.

"It feels good to be back on top, doesn't it?" Jack asked.

"It does," Barrows agreed. "Now if only the company knew the role our own Joe Friday played in all this. Kudos to you, old friend. You stuck your neck out for this company and nearly got it lopped off. Hewitt stock wouldn't be at its record high today without you."

"Not so fast," Jack said. "Not that I need it, but Susan Wright has decided she'd like to give Bob Laurence, Julie Sawyer, and me a little recognition after all. She asked me to prepare a few remarks for the annual all-employee meeting next week."

"Really?" Barrows said, his brows raised. "So I'll get to say I knew Jack Turner way back when. Very nice. Congratulations, buddy."

"Thanks," Jack said. "The only problem is, she wants me to keep the competitive intelligence stuff under wraps." Jack shook his head. "I wish I knew what everyone is so afraid of. A company should be applauded for having a CI function, not considered a pariah."

"So what will you say at the meeting?"

"I'm not sure yet. I guess I'll just keep it brief, make sure to heap praise on Julie, and try to let everyone know about the amazing work Laurence did for this company over the years. It's the least I can do. I just wish there was something more."

* * *

Hewitt Games celebrated its return to the top in style. The black-tie annual meeting was held at the Marriott, and there wasn't a seat left in the house.

Jack Turner proudly escorted his wife and Bob Laurence to the event. His emotions shifted from thrilled to terrified at the thought of addressing thousands of his peers.

After drinks and dinner, members of the executive team took to the stage to make their remarks. The message was much the same from each speaker: Howard Hewitt had built an amazing company, and Susan Wright was taking it to new heights.

When Wright finally took the podium to a three-minute standing ovation, Jack felt his palms begin to sweat.

"Got any jokes?" Laurence asked as the applause began to fade.

"Jokes?" Jack replied.

"You know, an icebreaker for your speech."

"I'm supposed to have an icebreaker?"

"You don't?" Laurence said, looking shocked.

Jack waved Laurence off as Wright began her address. She thanked all the speakers who had come before her for their kind words, and she asked if anyone remembered the first time she spoke to Hewitt's employees in a conference call just after Howard's death.

"I told you then that Howard Hewitt's greatest accomplishment was in hiring all of you and creating the best team in the industry," she said to a thunderous ovation. "And I also said that it was all of you—not Howard Hewitt, and not me—that were the key to the success of this organization, in the past, in the present, and in the future."

After another round of applause, Wright continued, "There are so many of you to thank, so many of you that have done so much for this organization. But tonight, I would like to point out one individual in particular."

Jack didn't feel the pat on the back from Laurence or the kiss on the cheek from Sofia. His body was numb.

"Many of you know Jack Turner as the director of our market research department," Wright said, pausing for the applause. "I know Jack Turner as the man who likes to drop bombshells in my lap."

Laughter filled the air. Laurence leaned over and whispered, "Icebreaker."

Jack smiled, but he sensed Wright was taking her speech in an unexpected direction.

"Not once last year but twice, Jack came to me with urgent information about our biggest competitor, Sampson Electronics. And on both occasions, I truly believe Jack helped save Hewitt from finally getting run over by the competition. For you see, Jack isn't merely a traditional market research practitioner. He's also a practitioner of competitive intelligence."

"She's doing it," Laurence said, sounding stunned as a confused murmur rose in the crowd. "She's actually doing it."

CHAPTER 28

EMBRACING CI

"I know what your initial reaction is," Susan Wright continued as the hall once again fell silent. "Because that was my initial reaction as well—great, our company engages in dumpster diving and wiretapping. That is, after all, the image the words 'competitive intelligence' conjure up, right?"

Uneasy laughter filled the hall. "But let me assure you, all of the competitive intelligence activities this company takes part in are 100 percent legal and ethical. And if they weren't, there is no way this great company would ever have anything to do with it."

Wright's words were powerfully delivered, the force of them seemingly lifting the haze that had settled over the audience. The crowd responded with applause.

"Our economy, our prices, our product offerings, and our entire free-enterprise system demand and require that we understand the competition. Don't they? And if it wasn't for competition, how would our goods and services become more affordable? How would new and enhanced technologies spring to market sooner, how and why would new services be created, and how else would consumers have the options and choices we all enjoy? Our economic system demands that we study our competitors just as much as we study our customers, if not more. We would be doing our consumers and ourselves a disservice if we didn't. That is what real competitive intelligence is about. And let me assure you all, there is nothing to be afraid of."

Wright paused for brief applause and gathered herself before continuing. "Tonight, I'm proud to stand before you as the leader of this great company and enthusiastically say yes, of course we look at our competitors," she said, her voice beginning to rise. "That is what helped make Howard Hewitt great, that is what helped make his company great, and it is what will continue to make this company even greater in the future."

In an instant, the crowd was on its feet, cheering wildly. Jack turned to look at Laurence and saw the old man misty-eyed and beaming.

"Now, about that Jack Turner," Wright said, laughing along with the crowd. "Jack, if you could please come up here and join me onstage."

Another round of applause filled the hall as Jack kissed his wife and then made his way to the stage. He stood in the bright lights next to his CEO, his heart racing in his chest.

"Jack, it was you who had the courage to tell me all about competitive intelligence, and it was you who did the hard work, studying our biggest competitor and finding the intelligence we needed to get us back on top. This company owes you a debt of gratitude. In thanks, and as a sure sign of this company's enthusiastic embrace of competitive intelligence now and going forward, I would like to offer you the role of Hewitt Games' first chief competitive officer."

Jack wasn't sure if he was standing on stage or on air. Was this really happening?

"I'm including a 1.5 million-dollar budget for your new department in this year's budget, and I'm giving you approval to hire up to four new analysts.

"All right, Jack!" Andy Barrows yelled in his all-too-familiar voice, spurring another round of applause from the crowd.

Wright gave Jack a handshake and then a hug, and she stepped aside for Jack to take the podium.

"Wow," Jack said, taking a moment to clear his thoughts. "And Susan said *I* was the one who likes to drop bombshells." After a warm laugh, Jack continued. "So I don't start babbling, I'll get this out as quickly as possible. First, yes, I would be honored to become Hewitt's CCO. Thank you, Susan Wright, for having the courage and vision to embrace competitive intelligence. I promise all of you that your CI team will work tirelessly to pull together extraordinary insights that positively impact our company's decision making. Second, Julie Sawyer, thank you for your hard work and for never saying, 'That's not my job.' I would be honored if you would become an analyst on our CI team. Third, I will actually be Hewitt Games' second chief competitive officer. The first was Bob Laurence, the man who brought competitive intelligence to this company over twenty years ago and spent nearly his entire career making sure Hewitt's roof was repaired while the sun was still shining. Thank you, Bob. None of this would have been possible without you."

As Jack left the stage to an audience of smiles and another ovation, there was no doubt about it: he was walking on air. It wasn't just because of the recognition or the huge promotion; it was because Bob Laurence finally got his due.

CHAPTER 29

JUST GETTING STARTED

Jack Turner made his way up to the Forty-Second on Monday morning, not for a meeting with the board or with Susan Wright—he was headed to his new office.

Ironically, Jack had been told that he would be occupying the same office that Bob Laurence once used. Jack carried his box of pictures, keepsakes, and supplies into his new home away from home and beamed—the view of the city was breathtaking. And it was all Jack's. What a year it had been.

After getting settled, Jack logged in on his computer and laughed when he saw that the first e-mail message of the day was from Laurence himself:

Jack:

I just knew you were the right person for the job. Howard would be proud.

As you've learned, competitive intelligence is an essential component in any successful business. Don't ever forget that, and don't ever back down. Always fight for CI. Without it, Hewitt would be just another "me too" company.

Once you've spent a few minutes enjoying the view in your new office (nice, isn't it?), you'll ask yourself, what now? Tough to say. There is so much more for you to learn about CI. Why don't you drop me a line, and we'll go over mining internal sources for CI leads? Then we can begin talking about integrating CI throughout Hewitt Games.

Roll up your sleeves, Jack. The hard work has just begun.

Respectfully,

Bob

PS: Don't ever forget, it wasn't raining when Noah built the Ark, and now it's your job to make sure Hewitt's roof is repaired while the sun is still shining.

AFTERWORD

WHAT'S EVERYONE SO AFRAID OF?

What's everyone so afraid of? Like Jack Turner, many in the business world are convinced that competitive intelligence is just a kinder, gentler name for corporate espionage. Nothing could be farther from the truth.

No doubt, over the years some people have engaged in practices that have abused ethics and put their companies at risk, under the banner of competitive intelligence. But isn't it true that every function within an organization has the potential to put the company at risk if guidelines, rules, ethics, laws, and good old common sense are ignored?

Think about it: should accounting be viewed as a pariah because an alarming number of organizations have cooked the books? Should marketing and advertising be completely ignored because countless organizations have been less than honest about their products and services, sometimes with drastic results? Of course not. It's not the functions themselves that are the problem, but rather the people within those functions who choose to ignore legal and ethical standards.

When conducted properly, competitive intelligence is a legal and ethical tool that actually helps *reduce* risk by uncovering critical information that senior executives can use to improve decision-making. In today's hyper-competitive business environment, that's something that every organization needs.

As Jack Turner learned, there is nothing to be afraid of when it comes to competitive intelligence. It's time to pull competitive intelligence out of the shadows and embrace it as a legitimate and necessary tool that's essential to the success of any business.

ABOUT THE AUTHORS

Gary D. Maag has been a leader in the research community for over two decades, with twenty-two years dedicated specifically to competitive intelligence. He has assisted dozens of Fortune 500 companies in high-profile business intelligence engagements. The Strategic and Competitive Intelligence Professionals (SCIP) awarded him the Catalyst Award for his contributions to the profession. He is the founder of the graduate-level CI program at Dominican University in Illinois and is the co-founder and CEO of Proactive Worldwide.

David J. Kalinowski is a twenty-two-year veteran in the CI field and co-founder and president of Proactive Worldwide. He has directed CI research for hundreds of domestic and international corporations, and he assists numerous advisory and executive boards with highly sensitive CI strategy development and training initiatives. He has been a recipient of SCIP's Catalyst Award, and he previously served on the SCIP board of directors.

Learn more about Proactive Worldwide at www.proactiveworldwide.com.